S0-BKW-157

CALIFORNIA THROUGH FOUR CENTURIES

CALIFORNIA
THROUGH
FOUR CENTURIES

*A Handbook of Memorable
Historical Dates*

By PHIL TOWNSEND HANNA

With a Foreword by
HERBERT EUGENE BOLTON

Drawings by
RAYMOND P. WINTERS

FARRAR & RINEHART, *Inc.*

On Murray Hill   New York

FOREWORD

ALL readers and students of California history will be grateful to Mr. Hanna for this book. "When did it happen?" is asked almost as frequently as "Who's Who?" No other reference work on the subject will give the answer so surely, so quickly, or so intelligently as this one. You know of an event but forget or never knew just when it took place. This book will tell you.

In CALIFORINA THROUGH FOUR CENTURIES the author has taken a broad view of history and assembled an amazing variety of interesting and important data; and he has shown prodigious industry in his search for accurate information. One will find in the work not alone answers to questions about the conventional topics usually found in text-books. It will tell to a day and at a glance when Father Crespí died; when the treaty of Guadalupe was signed; when the first camel corps reached Los Angeles; or when Amelia Earhart Putnam completed the first solo flight from Hawaii to California.

Most books on our State's history stop before the end of the nineteenth century. One-fifth of this volume treats of twentieth-century events. Here one may learn exactly when the Southern Pacific Coast Line was opened; when the largest tree in the world was discovered; when the golden poppy was made the State flower; when the Pacific cable to Guam was officially opened; when the first automobile crossed the continent under its own power—in only fifty-two days; or when the gates were closed and the storage of water was begun at Boulder Dam (February 1, 1935).

Though cyclopedic in form, the book is not a mere dictionary. The author has long been a student and writer of California history, and he understands its meaning. His brilliant Introduction and his pungent chapter over-views together form a penetrating interpretation of the events treated in the separate paragraphs. His fine literary style and his keen sense of values make even the detached items brimful of human interest. Read consecutively, the book gives a continuous and surprisingly complete account of California's significant and colorful past. I predict for it a gratifying reception.

HERBERT E. BOLTON.

Berkeley, California.
March 31, 1935.

INTRODUCTION

B ACK of every Californian, be he native or adopted, is a noble lineage. In a little more than a century and a half California has risen from a land of barbarians to become one of the most progressive commonwealths in the world. In it has developed a true aristocracy, founded on an extraordinary if not phenomenal record of individual and collective achievement. To the purple have ascended the lowly as well as the mighty; the weak and the strong; the man of brain and the man of brawn; the artist and the craftsman; the husbandman and the merchant. "What can you do?" and not "Who are you?" has been the question that has determined the qualifications of individuals to join the royal company.

The advancement of California can readily be traced through a number of distinct periods, and the thread of each is impressively apparent in the fabric of the State today.

The Spanish *conquistadores* who first came to California found a low social order indeed. The Indians were a debased race, little advanced from the anthropoid ape. It is doubtful if more primitive savages existed at that time on the face of the earth. Undoubtedly they comprised the weaker element in the successive tides of migration that swept into North America from Asia by way of the Bering Sea. They were the unfit that dropped out by the way as the mass of the stronger surged southward through Mexico, Central and South America, to establish the stalwart cultures of the Aztec, the Maya, and the Inca.

The favorable environment of California gave those left behind a new lease on life. But it was only temporary. It merely slowed down the rate of decay. Within them was the ineradicable germ of disintegration. Many sentimental reproaches have been hurled at the Spanish missionaries and colonists in California. They exterminated the Indian it is frequently asserted. This is dubious. They undoubtedly hastened the process, but the California Indian would have perished just the same had the Spaniards not come to these shores.

The Spaniards found the ground cleared, as it were, for the sowing of a new culture. They utilized the remnants of energy remaining among the passing Indians to impose their new order and, once established, the new order thrived. The Spaniards brought to California the romanticism, the imagination, and the appreciation of beauty that is inherent in their race. Their contribution to the ultimate culture was a basic and an important one. Modern Californians owe them much for the qualities they contributed, just as the later-coming Anglo-Saxons must be credited for their contributions of courage and thrift, their tolerance and fetishlike sense of justice; and the Orientals, for their industry and tenacity.

But above all these diverse attributes there was a common and a dominant element, the almost universal receptivity which they evinced toward new ideas and new ideals, and their flair for experimentation. Without this the culture could hardly have advanced at all; certainly it would never have reached its present eminent position.

The American conquest ushered in the second major influence, economically, politically, and sociologically, in the course of the State's destiny. The conquest, portentous though it was in the realm of world statesmanship, meant little in a material way to California. The land remained basically pastoral for two years. Then came James Wilson Marshall's discovery of gold in Sutter's Mill at Coloma—and the mad years of the gold rush with its lustful devastation and its devouring passions.

Subsequently there followed the peaceful invasion of sober and sane agronomists, determined to capitalize their labors in an uncommonly fertile land.

In preparing this compendium of memorable California dates, the plan has been to trace the development of California from its earliest recorded historical annals to the present time. The most valid criticism that has been hurled against the historians since the days of Herodotus has been that they have concerned themselves more with chronicling the exact dates of wars and of conquests, of the birth of kings and the elevation of potentates, and less with the influences that primarily motivated the subjugation of peoples and the modifications of social, political, and economic movements. I have, on sundry occasions, voiced similar objections to the presentation of California's history.

In essaying a book of this character, I am probably
somewhat inconsistent, for this is a date book, purely
and simply—a handbook designed to reveal readily and
quickly the highlights of California's annals through
four centuries. There are times when the lay reader, no
less than the student, wants to determine precisely the
date of some important occurrence, whether for the
mere satisfaction of knowing it or for the pursuit of
the study of comparative history.

In compiling such works as this, the temptation at
the outset and throughout its development is to make
it either inclusive or exclusive—to bring within it a
mass of inconsequential information of no possible
value in showing the significant episodes in the progress of the State or to confine it to those occurrences
that obviously determine the course of the Commonwealth. I have tried rather to follow a middle ground,
to include all of the obviously important dates and such
others as have, in my estimation, proved more or less
decisive, though they normally are overlooked by historians.

The dates of many decisive occurrences will be found
missing, for no events have been included that could
not be traced to an exact year, month, and day. Fortu-
nately, the bulk of these elusive dates are not really
significant. It would be interesting to know, of course,
the exact day when Hernando de Alarcón landed from
his little boat on the west bank of the Colorado River
and thus became the first white man to stand on the
soil of the present State of California. It would be interesting to know this, for Alarcón antedated Cabrillo's

arrival by two years, but it wouldn't be important, for he didn't take possession of the land and retired with little formality.

It would be interesting, too, to know precisely when the missionary fathers planted the grape, the orange, the fig, and the olive, but these dates wouldn't be important either, for from none of them sprang the modern horticultural industries that have meant so much to the economic advancement of the State.

Would that it were possible to know, though, just when William Wolfskill planted his first orchard of citrus fruits in Los Angeles, and when the first wine grapes were set out in the great dry valleys of the north! But these dates remain behind the veil, and they probably always shall.

It would be interesting, again, merely as a matter of curiosity, to know the exact date when David Douglass, the Scotch botanist, in removing for shipment to England the tiny specimens of firs that later were to be named for him, found enough gold intermingled with their roots to make a watch case. But this date wouldn't be especially important either, though it was the first recorded discovery of gold in California. It would hardly be more important than the discovery of gold in Placerita Canyon, the date of which we now know, for neither Douglass' discovery nor the Placerita find caused the slightest ripple in the serene and stately progress of the Commonwealth.

We know the name and the date of the arrival of the first American in California and of the first American permanently to settle here, but we are not precisely informed as to when American overland migration was initiated over the Gila River route, though we do know that the Wolfskill-Yount party arrived in Los Angeles from Taos in February, 1831, and that they were followed by the Jackson party, including that grand old pioneer, J. J. Warner, who arrived in San Diego in November of the same year.

How unfortunate, too, that we can't tell just what day in November, 1833, Joseph Reddeford Walker, with a party of trappers from Great Salt Lake, arrived in Monterey, after proceeding to Pyramid Lake, through the Carson Valley, up the Walker River, and across the Sierra near the headwaters of the Merced.

Equally unfortunate is the paucity of knowledge about Richard Henry Dana's movements on the coast of California. True enough, we know that the author of *Two Years Before the Mast* reached Santa Barbara first in January, 1835, but just when, and the dates of his subsequent journeyings, remain a mystery. Possibly the future may vouchsafe these and other illuminating facts.

No work of this character can ever be complete. This one doesn't pretend to be so. Month by month students are delving further and further back into the archives, disclosing new slants on California. All over the world hitherto unsuspected sources of information about California are revealing themselves. In the musty archives of Spain and of Latin America, of France, Germany, and England, of Russia and the Orient, there are constantly being found invaluable references by travelers and scientists, skilled and otherwise, to various episodes in California's advancement. In some of these, one day, we may find the data that will enable us to fill out the scheme of our traditions and our history, and permit us thus to gain a more detailed and satisfactory appraisal of our heritage.

The dates included in this handbook have been extracted from the most reliable of existing sources. For more than three years I have pursued the standard historical works and extended my researches to original unpublished documents, letters, and manuscripts. Files of newspapers covering more than fifty years have been minutely scanned. Frequently entire volumes would be read without securing a single date, when, on the contrary, one short manuscript would produce a score.

Foremost among the authorities consulted, of course, was the mighty Hubert Howe Bancroft, whose seven-volume *History of California* will doubtless always be the primary printed source of knowledge about the State. I have carefully read these seven volumes from cover to cover, including the voluminous and formidable footnotes and the equally confusing and prepossessing *Pioneer Register*—an achievement, I venture to say, not hitherto accomplished by any one else living. Other of Bancroft's numerous works disclosed noteworthy facts, especially his *Popular Tribunals, History of the Northwest Coast, California Pastoral,* and *California Inter Pocula.* No little information was gained from Bancroft's rare and seldom-encountered supplementary work, *Chronicles of the Builders of the Commonwealth.*

Rich in information about the Spanish period were

the various diaries of the Anza expeditions, and Father
Francisco Palóu's *New California,* both produced under
the editorship of Herbert Eugene Bolton, and Palóu's
Life of Father Junípero Serra. For the journeys of the
Spanish mariners, Henry R. Wagner's *Spanish Voyages
to the Northwest Coast in the Sixteenth Century*
proved of the greatest aid.

Invaluable for its many references to incidents of
post-gold days, was Theodore Henry Hittell's *History
of California* (though this estimable historian insists
the city of Los Angeles was founded on September 1,
1781, rather than September 4). Earlier historical
works, such as Robert T. Greenhow's *The History of
Oregon and California* and Alexander Forbes' *A History
of Upper and Lower California,* were of little service.
Such recollections as William Heath Davis' *Sixty Years
in California* and Alfred Robinson's *Life in California
before the Conquest,* meritorious though they are in
their class, were valueless for this compilation.

Publications consulted included various magazines
and periodicals—*Overland Monthly, Land of Sunshine,
Out West, The Golden Era, Hutching's California
Magazine,* and the, alas! often inconsistent files of various historical societies. Valuable for a number of items
were the *Quarterlies of the California Historical Society,* the publications of the Pacific Coast Academy of
History and *The Sierra Club Bulletin.*

Every issue of the *Los Angeles Times* for the past
forty-five years was meticulously examined for news
of contemporary events. Many have been included in
this chronology; many more omitted, for an event that

was headline news for a day or a week becomes of no historical significance in the comparative perspective of a year or a decade.

For material assistance in making available rare sources and in the settling of controversial points I am indebted to many whose aid and counsel I gratefully acknowledge. Notable among these are Mabel R. Gillis, California State Librarian; Laura C. Cooley, the Los Angeles Public Library; Robert Ernest Cowan, librarian and bibliographer; and Dr. Owen C. Coy, of the Department of History, University of Southern California. To Doctors Henry Raup Wagner and Frederick Webb Hodge, no less than to Robert Glass Cleland, I owe much for their stimulating friendship and their generous advice and assistance. And finally, I pay my respects to my able assistants, the Misses Kay Turbeville and Patrice Manahan.

CONTENTS

PART I

CONQUISTADORES
(1540–1822)

PART I

CONQUISTADORES

(1540–1822)

QUESTING for fair women, rare jewels and gold. . . .
For the mythical Straits of Anian and a short
route to India. . . . For the fabulous Kingdom of Cibola.
. . . For El Dorado, "the gilded province," and for
Quivira with its traditional riches. These were the goals
of the *conquistadores*. These were the phantoms that
beckoned hardy, bearded soldiers of the Spanish crown
over repellent and unknown deserts and mountains,
and lured doughty, courageous mariners with their
miniature vessels into the hazards of strange seas.

With the Crown went the Cross to subjugate barbarians for God and for King, to implant Christianity
and civilization among savages, to extend the temporal
domain of enterprising monarchs, and to further the
heavenly glory of the Lord of Hosts.

An incredible company these conquerors . . . noble
adventurers marching hard by lowly soldiers . . . cruel
and ruthless crusaders spreading their pallets beside
kindly, pious, zealous men of God. Seeking Loreleis
that never appeared, they found, in their stead, California, a vineyard fair and promising to their cause.
Ad majoram Dei gloriam!

3

May 9, 1540—Hernando de Alarcón, with two ships, left Acapúlco, Mexico, to coöperate with the land expedition of Francisco Vásquez de Coronado seeking the Seven Cities of Cibola. He ascended the Gulf of California along the western shore and reached the mouth of the Colorado River August 17 or 18. On the 26th he went up the river with small boats, seeking news of Coronado. In the vicinity of the junction of the Gila he disembarked on the western shore of the river. Thus he was the first white man to set foot on the soil of the present State of California, though Juan Rodríguez Cabrillo is credited with the discovery of the State.

September 28, 1542—Juan Rodríguez Cabrillo, a Portuguese navigator in the service of Spain and discoverer of California, commanding two vessels, the *San Salvador* and the *Victoria,* entered and discovered the present San Diego Bay, naming it "San Miguel." Cabrillo and some of his men went ashore and engaged in a skirmish with the Indians, three of the whites being wounded.

October 7, 1542—Cabrillo discovered the present Santa Catalina and San Clemente islands. He went ashore on one of them, though it is not known which. He named the former "San Salvador" and the latter "Victoria," after the two vessels under his command.

October 8, 1542—Cabrillo discovered Santa Monica Bay, which he called "Bahia de los Fumos" (Bay of the Smokes) because of the many camp-fires of the Indians seen there.

October 10, 1542—Cabrillo discovered Pueblo de las Canoas, an extensive village of Indians on the mainland of the Santa Barbara Channel. The village has been located at various points from San Buenaventura to Mugu Lagoon. Here Cabrillo held a colloquy with the Indians and took formal possession of the land for the King of Spain.

October 13, 1542—Cabrillo discovered Anacapa and Santa Cruz islands but failed to name them.

October 15, 1542—Cabrillo sighted the present Santa Cruz, Santa Rosa, and San Miguel islands. They were thought to be one island and were named "San Lucas." In January, 1543, the error was discovered. Thereupon the present Santa Cruz Island was named "San Salvador" (the same name formerly given to Santa Catalina); the present San Miguel, "La Posesión"; and the present Santa Rosa, "San Lucas."

October 18, 1542—Cabrillo discovered the present Point Concepción, which he named "Cape Galera."

November 11, 1542—Cabrillo discovered the present Santa Lucia Mountains, which he called the "Sierras de San Martín," in virtue of the fact that they were sighted on Saint Martin's Day.

November 16, 1542—Cabrillo sighted the present Monterey Bay, which he called "Bahia de los Pinos," or "Bay of the Pines."

November 18, 1542—Cabrillo named the Coast Range the "Sierras Nevadas." The name, identifying the present Sierra, first appears on the map of Father Pedro Font in 1777.

January 3, 1543—Cabrillo died at La Posesión (Cuyler's Harbor) on the present San Miguel Island, from a broken arm, probably infected, which he suffered during a shore journey on the island. Before he died he transferred command of the expedition to Bartolomé Ferrelo, who had acted as his chief pilot and whom he charged to continue the exploration so auspiciously begun. Cabrillo was buried on San Miguel, though his grave never has been found. One of Ferrelo's first acts was to name San Miguel "Isla de Juan Rodríguez," a name that proved ephemeral.

February 28, 1543—Bartolomé Ferrelo, who succeeded to command of the Cabrillo expedition on the latter's death, sailed to the northernmost point of his explorations, reaching $42\frac{1}{2}°$ in the vicinity of the present Rogue River, Oregon. From this point he returned to Mexico.

June 15, 1579—Sir Francis Drake, pious English buccaneer, commanding *The Golden Hind,* landed at Drake's Bay, north of the present San Francisco. Drake took possession of the land for England by setting up a post and nailing a sixpence to it. He christened his discovery "New Albion." While on shore he held a religious service which is the first recorded Christian religious service to be held in California.

November 4, 1595—Sebastián Rodríguez Cermeño, a Portuguese mariner in the service of Spain, commanding the *San Agustín* under orders to survey ports on the northwest coast of America that might afford protection to the Manila galleons, sighted California in the vicinity of Cape Mendocino.

December 8, 1595—Cermeño, with the *San Agustín,* was wrecked in the present Drake's Bay, which he called "San Francisco Bay." Taking to a small boat, he proceeded southward, missed the Golden Gate, and sighted (though he did not land) the present Bay of Monterey, which he called "San Pedro Bay."

November 10, 1602—Sebastián Vizcaíno, commanding three ships, the *San Diego,* the *Santo Tomás,* and the *Tres Reyes,* anchored in the present San Diego Bay and named it in honor of San Diego de Alcalá, whose feast is celebrated November 12. On the 12th, virtually the entire company went ashore, where mass was said by the Carmelite missionaries who accompanied Vizcaíno—Fathers Andrés de la Asumpción, Antonio de la Ascensión, and Tomás de Aquino. Cabrillo previously had called the port "San Miguel."

November 24, 1602—Vizcaíno discovered Santa Catalina Island, giving it the name it now bears. At Santa Catalina, Vizcaíno anchored near the middle of the eastern coast, going ashore on the 28th and trading with the Indians.

November 30, 1602—Members of Vizcaíno's expedition in a small launch entered San Pedro Bay, which they called "San Andrés," and discovered what long was known as Deadman's Island, but which they called "Isla vaja de buena gente."

December 2, 1602—Vizcaíno discovered Santa Barbara and San Nicolás islands, giving them the names they now bear, and trading with the Indians who came offshore in canoes.

December 16, 1602—Vizcaíno anchored in Monterey Bay. On the next day he landed and mass was said by the friars. The port was named "Monterey" in honor of Gaspar de Zuñiga y Acevedo (Count of Monterey),

Ninth Viceroy of Mexico. One hundred and sixty-eight years later, Monterey became the site of the principal presidio, as well as the capital of California, and the location of the chief mission in the chain of such establishments founded by the Franciscan missionaries.

January 3, 1603—Vizcaíno discovered the Carmel River, which he named "Río del Carmelo," in honor of the Carmelite friars who accompanied his expedition.

November 21, 1701—Father Eusebio Francisco Kino, Jesuit founder of the missions of Pimería Alta, crossed the Colorado River in the vicinity of Yuma and entered the present State of California to preach the Christian doctrine to the Indians, and to discover that Baja California was a peninsula and not an island. This was the first and only time Kino ever stood on the soil of the present California.

April 11, 1769—The *San Antonio,* with Don Juan Pérez as captain, bearing the first contingent of the sea division of the "sacred expedition" (there were four divisions in all; two by land and two by sea), charged by the Viceroy of New Spain, the Marquis de Croix, with the colonization of Alta California and the conversion of the Indians to the Catholic faith, arrived at San Diego, thus bringing to the State the first of its permanent colonists. Fathers Juan Vizcaíno and Francisco Gómez, Franciscan missionaries of the college of San Fernando in Mexico City, some subaltern officers, and a number of blacksmiths, carpenters, and other artisans sailed on the *San Antonio,* or *El Principe,* as it likewise was known. The vessel sailed from San José del Cabo, Baja California, on February 15, 1769.

April 29, 1769—The *San Carlos,* flagship of the sea division of the sacred expedition, with Don Vicente Vila as commander, arrived at San Diego. Aboard were Father Hernando Parrón, Franciscan missionary of the college of San Fernando in Mexico City; Lieut. Pedro Fages and twenty-five soldiers; Don Miguel Costansó, engineer and cosmographer; and Don Pedro Prat, surgeon. The *San Carlos* sailed from La Paz, Baja California, January 9, 1769, but unfavorable winds seriously delayed it, and it failed to reach San Diego until nineteen days after the *San Antonio* arrived. Many among the crew and the passengers were ill of scurvy.

May 14, 1769—The first contingent of the land division of the sacred expedition arrived at San Diego. The first contingent was under the military command of Capt. Fernando Rivera y Moncada and was accompanied by Father Juan Crespí, a Franciscan missionary of the college of San Fernando, in Mexico City. The party consisted, in addition to the above, of José Cañizares, engineer, twenty-five soldiers of the Company of the Royal Presidio of Loreto, three muleteers, and forty-two neophyte Indians. The company was assembled at Vellicatá in Baja California and set forth March 24, 1769.

May 17, 1769—The first permanent settlement in California was started when soldiers and sailors under command of the sacred expedition's officers, Vila, Rivera y Moncada, and Fages, moved from a temporary camp that had been established in New Town, San Diego, to North, or Old, San Diego, at the foot of the present Presidio Hill.

June 29, 1769—Don Gaspar de Portolá, governor of the Californias, arrived in San Diego in advance of the final contingent of the sacred expedition, which he commanded.

July 1, 1769—The second contingent of the land division of the sacred expedition reached San Diego. It was in charge of Don Gaspar de Portolá, commander-in-chief of the entire project and governor of the Californias. In the group was Father Junípero Serra, Franciscan missionary of the college of San Fernando in Mexico City and father-president of the missions of the Californias. Others in the party were Sergt. José Francisco Ortega, soldiers, muleteers, servants, and forty-four neophyte Indians. The company had been assembled from many points in Baja California at the recently-founded mission of San Fernando de Vellicatá, Baja California, which it left May 15, 1769.

July 14, 1769—Don Gaspar de Portolá, governor of the Californias, accompanied by Fathers Juan Crespí and Francisco Gómez, Lieut. Pedro Fages, Engineer

Miguel Costansó, twenty-seven soldiers, muleteers, and Christian Indians, left San Diego to discover the port of Monterey and locate sites for missions throughout California. Portolá stood on the shores of Monterey Bay on October 3 but failed to recognize it. He proceeded northward, where one of his subalterns discovered inner San Francisco Bay, then returned to San Diego, where he arrived January 4, 1770.

July 16, 1769—Father Junípero Serra founded the mission of San Diego de Alcalá, at Old Town, in San Diego, then called by the natives "Cosoy." This, the first of twenty-one missions to be established in Alta California, was named for Saint Diego of Alcalá, Spain, a Franciscan monk born at the beginning of the fifteenth century and who died November 12, 1463.

July 22, 1769—First Indians in California were baptized by Father Juan Crespí, at Los Cristianos, or Cañada del Bautismo, near the present community of San Clemente. The Indians, who were dying children of the Diegueño tribe, were given the Christian names of "María Magdalena" and "Margarita."

July 23, 1769—Don Gaspar de Portolá, seeking the port of Monterey, camped on the present site of San Juan Capistrano, which Father Juan Crespí called "the valley of Santa María Magdalena."

August 2, 1769—Portolá camped on the present site of Los Angeles. In view of the fact that the previous day marked the jubilee of Our Lady of the Angels of Porciúncula, Father Juan Crespí so christened it. Though the party here experienced three earthquakes, Crespí recorded that the site "has all the requisites for a large settlement."

August 3, 1769—Portolá camped on the site of the present Brea Pits in Los Angeles, thus being the first white man to discover oil in California. Father Juan Crespí called the location "the Spring of the Alders of San Estévan."

August 14, 1769—Portolá camped on the site of the present city of San Buenaventura, which Father Juan Crespí called "La Asunción de Nuestra Señora" because it was the eve of the Feast of the Virgin Mary.

August 17, 1769—Portolá camped on the site of the

present city of Carpinteria, the soldiers of the party giving it its present name. Father Juan Crespí called it "San Roque." Here, as at La Brea, the party noted oil deposits.

August 18, 1769—Portolá camped on the site of the present city of Santa Barbara, which Father Juan Crespí called "Laguna de la Concepción."

August 24, 1769—Portolá camped at the mouth of the present Gaviota Pass, which the soldiers called "La Gaviota" because they killed a sea-gull.

September 7, 1769—Portolá camped near the present city of San Luis Obispo at a point which was named "Cañada de los Osos" because the soldiers encountered a number of bears. The site is still so called.

October 3, 1769—Portolá, seeking the port of Monterey, reached Point of Pines, thus standing on the very rim of Monterey Bay without recognizing it.

October 8, 1769—Portolá camped on the present Pájaro River, which the soldiers so named because they found a bird which the Indians had stuffed.

October 18, 1769—Portolá crossed an arroyo at the

site of the present city of Santa Cruz which he so named.

November 2, 1769—Sergt. José Francisco Ortega, attached to the expedition of Gaspar de Portolá seeking Monterey Bay, discovered inner San Francisco Bay, though part of the bay may have been seen by other members of the Portolá party on October 31. Ortega failed to name the bay "San Francisco." The outer bay, under Point Reyes, had been known for some time.

December 7, 1769—A council was held by the Portolá expedition at its camp beyond the Carmel River near Point Lobos to determine whether to continue the search for Monterey or return to San Diego. It was determined that all should retreat, as supplies were running low. The party started south on December 10, retracing their northward path and reached San Diego on January 24, 1770.

April 16, 1770—The *San Antonio,* commanded by Juan Pérez and bearing Engineer Miguel Costansó and Father Junípero Serra, left San Diego to join Gaspar de Portolá and his land expedition and to effect the establishment of the presidio of Monterey. The vessel reached Monterey on May 31. After the establishment of the mission and presidio, the *San Antonio* sailed for San Blas.

April 17, 1770—Gaspar de Portolá left San Diego on his second expedition to seek the port of Monterey. He reached it (and recognized it, which he had failed to do on his first expedition) on May 24.

May 24, 1770—Portolá, Crespí, and Fages recognized

the port of Monterey, which they had seen but failed
to recognize during the first expedition in 1769.

June 3, 1770—Misión San Carlos de Monterey was
founded by Father Junípero Serra. The mission was
the second to be established in Alta California and was
named for Saint Charles Borromeo (1538-1584), Arch-
bishop of Milan and Papal Secretary of State under

Pius IV, who was one of the chief factors in the Catholic Counter-reformation. In 1771 the mission was
moved to its present site on the banks of the Río Carmelo and re-named "Misión San Carlos Borromeo del
Carmelo."

June 3, 1770—Gaspar de Portolá, governor of the
Californias, assisted by Father Junípero Serra and soldiers, founded the presidio of Monterey and took
formal possession of the land in the name of
Charles III, King of Spain. The formalities consisted
of the planting of the royal standard, the uprooting of
plants, and the casting of stones, the latter symboliz-
ing the seizing of the territory. The establishment of
the mission of San Carlos de Monterey, which in 1771

was moved to the Carmel River and re-named "San Carlos Borromeo del Carmelo," was coincidental. The presidio destined to be the capital of California was founded on the beach near the oak under which Sebastián Vizcaíno had claimed the land in 1603, and named it Monterey in honor of the Count of Monterey (Gaspar de Zuñiga y Acevedo), Ninth Viceroy of Mexico (1595-1603).

July 9, 1770—Leaving Pedro Fages in command, Gaspar de Portolá sailed on the *San Antonio* for Mexico, thus retiring as California's first governor. Of his life we know little. He was born in Balaguer, Catalonia, Spain, about 1723, became an ensign in the dragoon regiment of Villavigiosa in 1734, a lieutenant in 1743, and a captain in 1764. After leaving California he was appointed governor of the city of Puebla, Mexico, taking office February 23, 1777. He returned to Spain about 1784. Neither the date nor the place of his death are known. Portolá never liked California. He blundered badly in his search for Monterey and complained bitterly about the character of the country. Being out of sympathy with the colonization venture, as is evident from his journals, he doubtless was happy to leave it on the first opportunity.

November 21, 1770—Capt. Pedro Fages, with six soldiers and a muleteer, left Monterey for an exploration expedition that led him through the Santa Clara Valley, up the eastern shore of San Francisco Bay to the vicinity of the present city of Alameda and back to Monterey, which he reached December 4. Fages' journey was the first inland exploration undertaken from Monterey.

July 14, 1771—Misión San Antonio de Padua, third of the chain of missions to be founded by Franciscans in Alta California, was dedicated by Fathers Junípero Serra, Miguel Pieras, and Buenaventura Sitjar. The mission was named for Saint Anthony, founder of Christian monasticism (circa A.D. 250-350).

September 8, 1771—Misión San Gabriel Arcángel, fourth of the Franciscan missions in Alta California, was founded by Fathers Angel Somera and Pedro Benito Cambón. It was named for the Archangel Gabriel, "the angel of the Incarnation and of Consolation and of the Power of God."

March 20, 1772—Capt. Pedro Fages, accompanied by Father Juan Crespí and a company of soldiers, left the presidio of Monterey to explore the shores of San Francisco Bay by land. The party proceeded through Salinas, San Juan Bautista, and the Santa Clara Valley, thence up the east side of the bay through Berkeley and Richmond, across the western spur of Mt. Diablo to Pittsburg, from which point they passed southward through the present Livermore and Sunol valleys and back to Monterey, which was reached on April 5. These were the first whites to see the San Joaquín and Sacramento valleys.

April 30, 1772—A royal decree settled jurisdiction over the missions of the Californias by granting to the missionaries of the Dominican Order control of the establishments in Baja California, and to the Franciscans the management of those in Alta California.

September 1, 1772—Fathers Junípero Serra and José Cavaller founded Misión San Luís Obispo de Tolosa, fifth of the Franciscan missions of California. It was named for Saint Louis, Bishop of Toulouse (February, 1274–August 19, 1297), who entered the Franciscan Order after he had been confined for seven years in Tarragon and Barcelona as a hostage for his father, Charles II of Anjou.

October 20, 1772—Father Junípero Serra sailed from San Diego for Mexico to plead the cause of the California missions before a new viceroy and to protest against the plea of the Dominicans to be given equal jurisdiction over the missions. Serra arrived in Mexico City February 3, 1773. Here he met Viceroy Antonio María Bucareli y Ursua, whom he found greatly interested in the California project. Serra's representations resulted in the maintenance of the port of San Blas, which was to have been abandoned, the gaining of needed supplies, the removal of the unsympathetic Pedro Fages as governor of California, and the assignment of a group of artisans to the missions. Serra likewise induced Bucareli to authorize the first expedition of Juan Bautista de Anza to explore a land route between Sonora and California. His objects attained, Serra sailed from San Blas January 24, 1774, arriving at San Diego March 13, 1774.

August 19, 1773—The first California boundary was established when Father Francisco Palóu erected a cross defining the limits of Dominican and Franciscan territory, the former having been given jurisdiction over the missions of Baja California, and the latter over those of Alta California. Until a few years ago, the cross still stood on a knoll back of the Dominican mission of Nuestra Señora de Descanso, thirty miles south of Tijuana in the present Mexican territory of Baja California.

January 8, 1774—Capt. Juan Bautista de Anza left Tubac, Sonora, to explore an all-land route between the settlements on the mainland of Mexico and the presidios, pueblos, and missions of Alta California. He was accompanied by Fathers Francisco Garcés and Juan Díaz. He reached San Gabriel Mission on March 22 and Monterey on May 1—the first white man ever to make the journey from Sonora to the California coast by land.

March 22, 1774—Juan Bautista de Anza reached San Gabriel Mission on the first overland journey from Sonora to California.

June 11, 1774—Juan Pérez, commanding the *Santiago,* sailed from Monterey to explore and take possession of the northwest coast of America up to 60°. He reached the extremity of Queen Charlotte's Island, in 55°, then returned to Monterey and Mexico.

September 30, 1774—Don Felipe de Neve was appointed governor of California by Viceroy Antonio María Bucareli y Ursua. Neve succeeded Felipe de Barri who, as governor of Baja California, had assumed jurisdiction over Alta California on Portolá's departure in 1770. Barri never visited the northern territory, and his reign was marked by frequent and bitter clashes with the Franciscans.

March 16, 1775—Lieut. Bruno Heceta, with Juan Pérez as pilot, left San Blas, Mexico, in command of a second expedition to explore and take possession of the northwest coast of America. The expedition reached 49° on August 11, turned southward to Monterey, which was reached on August 29, and thence returned to Mexico. During the course of the expedition the port of Trinidad and the mouth of the Columbia River were discovered.

June 7, 1775—The Heceta-Pérez expedition, exploring the northwest coast of America, discovered Trinidad Bay, naming it and taking formal possession of the surrounding region for the King of Spain.

August 1, 1775—Juan Manuel de Ayala, commander of the *San Carlos,* entered San Francisco Bay in a small boat, accompanied by his pilots, José Cañizares and Juan Bautista Aguirre. The expedition, the first to sail the waters of the bay, eventually surveyed and mapped it, giving names to many of its landmarks, such as Angel Island, Alcatraz Island, and San Pablo Bay.

August 16, 1775—A Spanish Royal Decree established the capital of California at Monterey, with Felipe de Neve as governor.

September 29, 1775—Capt. Juan Bautista de Anza left San Miguel de Horcasitas, Sonora, on his second land expedition to California. With him were 240 colonists, destined to settle San Francisco; 165 mules, 304 horses, and 302 cattle. He was also accompanied by Fathers Pedro Font and Francisco Garcés. The caravan reached San Gabriel January 4, 1776, and San Francisco on March 28. Only one of the party died on the lengthy and arduous journey. In compensation, eight children were born en route. Anza's two expeditions to California show him to have been a courageous explorer and an excellent leader. Anza was born at Fronteras, Sonora, in 1735, the son of a frontier captain. He entered military service in 1752 and engaged in numerous campaigns against the Apaches, becoming commander of the presidio of Tubac in 1759. After his California journeys, Anza was appointed governor of New Mexico in 1778, serving until 1787, when he retired to Arispe, Sonora, where he died December 19, 1788.

November 4, 1775—Eight hundred wild Indians attacked San Diego Mission, seized Father Luís Jaume, disrobed him and beat him to death, and set fire to the mission structures. A carpenter, likewise, was slain, and six others wounded. In the quelling of the revolt, Fernando Rivera y Moncada was excommunicated by the priests for seizing from the church in which he had taken sanctuary a neophyte participant in the assault. Jaume thus became the first martyr in California, and Rivera y Moncada the first to be excommunicated.

December 9, 1775—Father Francisco Garcés left the expedition of Capt. Juan Bautista de Anza at the Laguna de Santa Olaya to travel alone among the Indians of Southern California, preaching Christianity. His travels took him to San Gabriel Mission, which he reached March 24, 1776, thence northward through the San Gabriel and Tehachapi mountains and the San Joaquín Valley as far north as Tulare Lake. From here he returned to the Mojave villages, down the Colorado, and finally reached his home mission of San Xavier del Bac, near the present Tucson, on September 17, 1776. Garcés carried with him a banner, one side depicting the beauties of Christianity; the other the horrors of paganism, which he showed to the aborigines.

December 24, 1775—Salvador Ignacio Linares, son of Ygnacio and Gertrudis Rivas Linares, was born at Middle Willows, near Warner Hot Springs. The boy was the first white child born in California. His parents were members of the expedition of Juan Bautista de Anza, sent to colonize San Francisco.

April 19, 1776—Don Felipe de Neve was instructed to transfer the capital of both Upper and Lower California to Monterey, and Fernando Rivera y Moncada was ordered to Loreto as lieutenant-governor. Neve arrived at Monterey February 3, 1777, to assume office.

September 17, 1776—The presidio of San Francisco was founded by Lieut. José Joaquín Moraga, assisted by Fathers Tomás de la Peña and Francisco Palóu. The day selected, on the Catholic calendar, is observed by the feast of the Impression of the Wounds of Saint Francis, patron saint of the new province. The customary formalities of raising flag and cross and taking possession in the name of Charles III, King of Spain, were observed.

October 9, 1776—Misión San Francisco de Asís, sixth of the Alta California missions established by the Franciscans, was founded by Fathers Francisco Palóu, Pedro Cambón, José Nocedal and Tomás de la Peña. It was named for Saint Francis of Assisi (circa 1181–October 3, 1286), founder of the Franciscan Order.

November 1, 1776—Fathers Junípero Serra and Gregorio Amurrio established Misión San Juan Capistrano, seventh Franciscan mission in Alta California.

It was previously founded on October 30, 1775, by Father Francisco Fermín de Lasuén and Lieut. José Francisco Ortega, but on November 7, 1775, was abandoned when news was received of the massacre at San Diego of Father Luís Jaume. It was named for Saint John Capistran (1385–October 23, 1456), a companion of Saint Bernardine of Siena and later a nuncio to the Holy See.

January 12, 1777—Misión Santa Clara, eighth Franciscan mission in Alta California, was founded by Father Tomás de la Peña. It was named for Saint Clare of Assisi (July 16, 1194–August 11, 1253), cofoundress of the Order of Poor Ladies, or Clares, and first Abbess of San Damiano.

November 29, 1777—San José de Guadalupe, first

pueblo or "city" in California, was founded by five colonists who had come with Juan Bautista de Anza, under supervision of José Joaquín Moraga.

June 1, 1779—Gov. Felipe de Neve drafted his subsequently famous *Reglamento,* approved October 24, 1781, by the King of Spain, providing a complete code of legislation for the province of the Californias. It detailed laws for the government of the presidios and regulated colonization. Under its provisions the pueblo of San José was reorganized and Los Angeles was established.

March 20, 1780—Comandante-general Teodoro de Croix issued instructions for the establishment of two missions on the California side of the Colorado River, in the vicinity of Yuma. The first of these was located opposite the present town of Yuma, was named "Misión La Purísima Concepción de María Santíssima," and was founded by Fathers Juan Antonio Barreneche and Francisco Garcés. The second mission, named "Misión San Pedro y San Pablo de Bicuñer," was founded some twelve miles down the river, near the present Pilot Knob, by Fathers Juan Díaz and Matías Moreno. Unlike the coastal missions, these establishments were a combination of mission, presidio and pueblo. Precisely when they were founded is not known, but it was some time late in 1780. The missions were abandoned after July 19, 1781, when hostile Yuma Indians massacred the four missionaries and twenty soldiers and fourteen civilians, including Capt. Fernando Xavier Rivera y Moncada. The latter were en route to found Los Angeles.

July 17, 1781—The Yuma Massacre, resulting in the deaths of Fathers Francisco Garcés, Juan Díaz, Juan Antonio Barreneche and José Matías Moreno, started at Misión San Pedro y San Pablo, and spread to Misión La Concepción. The following day the Indians attacked and slew Capt. Rivera y Moncada. All told, forty-six were killed.

September 4, 1781—El Pueblo de Nuestra Señora de Los Angeles de Porciúncula was founded under instructions from Gov. Felipe de Neve. The first colonists consisted of eleven families totalling forty-four men, women and children, chiefly *mestizos,* or half-breeds, Indian and Spanish, recruited from Sonora and Sinaloa.

September 16, 1781—An expedition under command of Lieut.-Col. Pedro Fages left the presidio of Pitic, Sonora, in a campaign against hostile Yuma Indians who, during the previous July, had massacred four priests and a number of soldiers at the then recently established missions of San Pedro y San Pablo de

Bicuñer and La Purísima Concepción, near the present Yuma. After several skirmishes with Indians under the Yuman chief, Palma, the casualties not being stated,

Fages buried the bodies of the slain priests and soldiers and proceeded overland to Misión San Gabriel, which he reached April 25, 1782.

January 1, 1782—Father Juan Crespí, companion of Fathers Serra and Palóu, and California's first and most extensive diarist, died at Misión San Carlos Borromeo, where his body was buried in the mission church on the gospel side of the presbytery. Crespí was born in 1721 on the Island of Mallorca, was a schoolmate of Palóu, was assigned to the college of San Fernando in Mexico in 1749, and in 1751 went to the missions of the Sierra Gorda. He arrived in Baja California in 1768, served temporarily at La Purísima, and in 1769 accompanied the first land division of the sacred expedition into Alta California. He accompanied Portolá's two expeditions to Monterey, and Fages' to the San Joaquín. He was one of the founders of Misión San Carlos, later was attached to Misión San Diego, and served as chaplain of the *Santiago*. He is regarded as an excellent diarist and an irreproachable priest.

March 31, 1782—Misión San Buenaventura was founded by Fathers Junípero Serra and Pedro Benito Cambón, as the ninth Franciscan mission in Alta California. It was named for Saint Bonaventure (1221–July 15, 1274), Doctor of the Church, cardinal-bishop of Albano and minister-general of the Friars Minor.

April 21, 1782—The presidio of Santa Barbara was founded by Gov. Felipe de Neve, but no mission was established until December 4, 1786.

July 12, 1782—Don Pedro Fages was appointed governor of the Californias and Felipe de Neve was promoted to the position of inspector-general of Provincias Internas. Neve was probably California's ablest Spanish governor. He was in full accord with the colonization policy, codified the regulations, and exercised an active and energetic interest in the pueblos founded thereunder. His preference for secular authority and organization brought him into frequent conflict with the missionaries. Little is known of Neve's early life. He was major of the Querétaro regiment of provincial cavalry from 1766 until he was chosen in 1774 to succeed Barri. He served in Sonora as inspector-general, with headquarters in Alamos, until his death, November 3, 1784.

August 28, 1784—Father Junípero Serra, father-president of the missions of California, died at Misión San Carlos Borromeo, where he was buried. Father Serra was born at Petra, on the island of Mallorca, Spain, November 24, 1713. He took the Franciscan habit at Palma, September 14, 1730, and made his profession September 15, 1731, when he took the name "Junípero" after a noted companion of Saint Francis. He taught in the convent of Palma and the Lucullian University, and on March 30, 1749, was assigned to the college of San Fernando in Mexico. He served in the Sierra Gorda missions from 1750 to 1759, then was assigned to the Apache missions on the Río San Sabá in Texas. With the expulsion of the Jesuits from Mexico in 1767, the Franciscans were given jurisdiction over

their former missions in Baja California, Serra becoming president July 14, 1767. There he labored for two years, leaving in 1769 to found the missions of Alta California. He personally established six of these—San Diego de Alcalá, San Carlos Borromeo, San Antonio de Padua, San Luís Obispo de Tolosa, San Juan Capistrano and San Buenaventura. "His laborious and exemplary life," his friend and biographer, Father Francisco Palóu, remarks, "is nothing but a beautiful field decked with every class of flowers of excellent virtues."

October 20, 1784—The first land grant in California

—Rancho San Rafael—was made by Gov. Pedro Fages to José María Verdugo. The grant covered portions of the present cities of Glendale and Burbank.

September 14, 1786—Jean François Galoup de la Pérouse, commanding the French frigates *Boussole* and *Astrolabe,* the first friendly foreign visitor of distinction to California, arrived in Monterey. La Pérouse stayed in California but ten days and saw only that part of it in the immediate vicinity of Monterey. Through gifts to the missionaries and the military officials, he introduced the potato to California, it is said. He provided an interesting and informative account of his observations—highly critical of the treatment of the Indians by the missionaries—in his *Voyages de la Pérouse autour du monde* in Paris in 1797, an English translation appearing in London in 1799.

December 4, 1786—Misión Santa Barbara was founded by Fathers Fermín Francisco Lasuén, Antonio Paterna and Cristóbal Orámas. It was the tenth of the missions founded in Alta California by the Franciscans, and was named for Saint Barbara, the daughter of a rich merchant of Heliopolis, Egypt, who, tradition has it, embraced Christianity in the third century and was beheaded. Her father, Dioscorus, was the executioner. Immediately after her death, the father was struck by lightning and killed. Saint Barbara is popularly regarded as the patron saint in time of thunderstorm and fire, and the protector of artillerymen and miners.

December 8, 1787—Misión La Purísima Concepción, eleventh Franciscan mission in Alta California, was founded by Father Fermín Francisco Lasuén. Because it was established on the day of the Feast of the Immaculate Conception it was so named.

December 9, 1789—Father José Cavaller, one of the founders with Father Serra, of Misión San Luís Obispo de Tolosa, died at the mission where he had served continuously since its founding. He was buried in the mission church. He was a native of the town of Falcet, in Catalonia, Spain. A Franciscan, he left the college of San Fernando in Mexico City in October, 1770, and reached California in March, 1771. He possessed the reputation for being a zealous and successful missionary.

April 16, 1791—Don José Antonio Romeu succeeded Pedro Fages as governor of California. He was appointed May 16, 1790, by Viceroy Revillagigedo. Fages, though an excellent soldier, was regarded as a tyrant by the missionaries. As military commander of Alta California he incurred the ire of the friars, and Serra secured his removal in 1774. When he returned as governor he brought with him his wife, Doña Eulalia de Callis, and his son. Of a tempestuous nature, the good offices of the priests were sought on numerous occasions to settle quarrels between her and the governor. In October, 1794, he was still living in Mexico City. When he died is not known.

September 13, 1791—A Spanish expedition under command of Alejandro Malaspina, in the corvettes *Descubierta* and *Atrevida,* engaged in an exploring voyage around the world, arrived at Monterey.

September 13, 1791—John Groehm (Graham), first American in California, attached to the exploring expedition of Alejandro Malaspina, arrived at Monterey. Groehm seems to have died and been buried on the day of his arrival.

September 25, 1791—Misión de Santa Cruz, or "the mission of the Holy Cross," twelfth Franciscan establishment in Alta California, was founded by Fathers Alonso Salazar and Baldomero López.

October 9, 1791—Misión de Nuestra Señora de la Soledad, or the "mission of Our Lady of Solitude," thirteenth Franciscan mission in California, was founded by Fathers Fermín Francisco Lasuén, Buenaventura Sitjar and Diego García.

April 9, 1792—Don José Joaquín de Arrillaga assumed the office of governor of California on the death of José Antonio Romeu. Romeu, a native of Valencia, Spain, had served as captain with Fages in Indian campaigns in Sonora before 1782. On his appointment as governor he was in command of the España Dragoon Regiment, with the rank of lieutenant-colonel. A competent administrator, Romeu had little chance to show his ability on account of ill-health. He died the day Arrillaga took office and was buried at Misión San Carlos.

November 14, 1792—Capt. George Vancouver, distinguished English explorer, commanding the sloop-of-war *Discovery,* arrived at San Francisco, on the first of three visits to California. He stayed at San Francisco for eleven days, then proceeded to Monterey, where he remained until January 14, 1793. On his second visit, Vancouver arrived at San Francisco on October 19, 1793, stayed five days, continued on to Monterey where he remained five days, and then proceeded down the coast to Santa Barbara, San Buenaventura and San Diego, sailing from the latter port December 9, 1793. On his third visit he was at Monterey November 6, 1794, and finally left California on December 2. In the intervals between his visits, he was engaged in the exploration of the northwest coast. He left two place-names on the southern coast of California—Point Fermin and Point Dume, named for Fathers Fermín Francisco Lasuén and Francisco Dumetz, both of whom he knew and admired. Like La Pérouse, he wrote extensively of California in his *A Voyage of Discovery to the North Pacific Ocean and Round the World,* published in London in 1798, and, like La Pérouse, he was critical of the mission system though hardly as harsh as his French contemporary.

February 13, 1793—Father Antonio Paterna, one of the founders of Misión Santa Barbara, died at the mission, where his body was buried. Paterna was a native of Seville, a Franciscan, and had served twenty years in the Sierra Gorda missions in Mexico before coming to California in 1771. Here he was attached successively to San Gabriel, San Luís Obispo and Santa Barbara. Paterna was acting president of the missions in 1772 and 1773. He was known as a faithful and devout worker.

May 14, 1794—Diego de Borica succeeded José Arrillaga (provisional) as governor of California, assuming office at Loreto.

October 29, 1796—The first American vessel to touch at a California port, the *Otter,* commanded by Capt. Ebenezer Dorr, anchored at Monterey. Dorr

secretly landed ten men and a woman—English convicts from Botany Bay who had smuggled themselves
aboard the *Otter*. The Spaniards were incensed at first,
but the convicts proved capable artisans and an asset
to the community until they were ordered sent to
Cádiz. Dorr was a northwest trader and visited
Monterey to replenish supplies before proceeding to
China.

June 11, 1797—Father Fermín Francisco Lasuén
founded Misión San José, fourteenth Franciscan establishment in Alta California. It was named for Saint
Joseph, spouse of the Virgin Mary and foster father of
Jesus of Nazareth.

June 24, 1797—Misión San Juan Bautista was
founded by Fathers Fermín Francisco Lasuén, José
Manuel Martiarena and Magín Catalá. It was the
fifteenth Franciscan mission in Alta California and was
named for Saint John the Baptist.

July 24, 1797—The Villa of Branciforte, named for
the Marques de Branciforte (Miguel de la Grua Tala-
manca), fifty-third viceroy of Mexico (1794-1798), was
founded by Gov. Diego de Borica. Laid out according
to the "Plan of Pitic" (on which the present city of
Hermosillo, Mexico, is built and which was believed to
be ideal for pueblos among potentially hostile savages),
Branciforte was to have been California's model city.
From the outset, however, the project was a failure.
The location—the present site of Santa Cruz—was not
attractive to colonists and crops did not thrive. The
villa languished, and a few years after its establishment
was all but forgotten.

July 25, 1797—Fathers Fermín Francisco Lasuén and Buenaventura Sitjar founded Misión San Miguel Arcángel, sixteenth Franciscan mission in Alta California. It was named for Saint Michael the Archangel, whose "name was the war-cry of the good angels in the battle fought in heaven against Satan and his followers."

September 8, 1797—Fathers Fermín Francisco Lasuén and Francisco Dumetz founded Misión San Fernando Rey de España, seventeenth of the Franciscan missions of Alta California. It was named for Saint Ferdinand III (1198–May 30, 1252), King of Leon and

Castile and a member of the Third Order of Saint Francis.

June 13, 1798—Fathers Fermín Francisco Lasuén, Antonio Peyri, and Juan José Norberto Santiago established Misión San Luís Rey de Francia, eighteenth Franciscan mission in Alta California. It was named for Saint Louis IX (April 25, 1215–August 25, 1270), King of France.

March 17, 1803—Capt. William Shaler with the

American ship, the *Lelia Bird,* arrived at San Diego—
the first commercial otter-hunting expedition to reach
California.

March 22, 1803—The crew of the *Lelia Bird* engaged
in otter-hunting with Capt. William Shaler as commander, participated in an artillery battle with the
Spanish soldiers stationed at the fort on Point Gui-
jarros at San Diego. The skirmish followed the arrest
and subsequent rescue of members of the ship's crew,
who had been arrested by Spanish authorities for trading in otter skins with the natives, contrary to the law.
Only one shot, out of perhaps a score, hit the ship, and
this only damaged the rigging. The vessel thereupon
escaped. There were no human casualties.

June 26, 1803—Father Fermín Francisco Lasuén,
founder of eight of the missions of Alta California—
Santa Barbara, La Purísima, Soledad, San José, San
Juan Bautista, San Miguel, San Fernando and San
Luís Rey—died at Misión San Carlos, where his body
was buried. Lasuén was a native of Vitoria, Alava,
Spain. He came to Baja California in 1768 and to Alta
California in 1773. He was elected president of the
California missions to succeed Serra in 1785. Lasuén
was an indefatigable worker, a devout priest, a competent administrator and a kindly man. Some historians regard him as the greatest of all the missionaries ever to have labored in Alta California. His founding of eight of the twenty-one missions made for him a
record in this respect.

March 4, 1804—A royal decree of the King of Spain
partitioned California into Upper California and Lower

California, and established the capital of the former at Monterey, with José Joaquín de Arrillaga as governor.

March 26, 1804—Don José Joaquín de Arrillaga by royal order was confirmed as governor of California. Arrillaga had occupied the office once before on the death of Romeu, and in the present instance had served as ad interim governor since 1799, when Diego de Borica was relieved of his duties in the office at his own request. Borica is known as one of the kindest and wittiest of California's Spanish governors. A bon vivant, he entertained lavishly and maintained unusually cordial relations with the friars. Of his antecedents little is known, save that he was a Knight of Santiago and a wealthy and cultured man. Borica died at Durango, July 19, 1800.

September 17, 1804—Fathers Estévan Tapis, José Antonio Calzada, Marcelino Ciprés and Romualdo Gutiérrez founded Misión Santa Inés, Virgin y Mártir, nineteenth Franciscan mission in California. The mission was named for Saint Agnes of Assisi, who lived in the thirteenth century, was a sister of Saint Clare and one of the first to embrace the religious life under the Rule of Saint Francis, as a Poor Clare or Minoress.

February 9, 1806—Father Tomás de la Peña, founder of Misión San Francisco de Asís, died at the college of San Fernando, in Mexico City, while acting as guardian. De la Peña, a native of Spain, arrived in California from Mexico in 1772, being attached successively to Misión San Diego, San Luís Obispo, San Carlos, and Santa Clara. He returned to Mexico in 1794. Though an able missionary, he is said to have been hot-tempered and harsh in his treatment to neophytes.

April 5, 1806—Chamberlain Nikolai Petrovich Rezánof, imperial inspector of Russian establishments in Alaska, and G. H. Von Langsdorff, aulic counsellor to the Emperor of Russia, arrived in San Francisco on the *Juno* with a cargo of Russian goods, seeking food for starving Sitka and trade in otter skins. Rezánof fell in love with Concepción Argüello, daughter of the commander of the San Francisco presidio. She promised to marry him and shortly thereafter he set out across Siberia to gain his Tsar's consent. During the journey he died. Concepción didn't learn of his death until years later. When she did she entered a convent at Benicia. The romance is commemorated in a heroic poem by Bret Harte and in Gertrude Atherton's novel, *Rezánov*.

July 19, 1806—Father José María Zalvidea and Lieut. Francisco Ruíz left Misión Santa Barbara to explore the San Joaquín Valley. The party proceeded to Santa Inés, thence across the Coast Range, skirting the northern end of Buena Vista Lake and the southern shores of the then-existing Laguna de las Tulares (Tulare Lake), reaching its northernmost point in the vicinity of the present Visalia. Thence it returned southward through the Tejon or Tehachapi Pass to Misión San Gabriel, which was reached August 14.

September 21, 1806—An exploring expedition, under command of Alférez Gabriel Moraga and Father Pedro Muñoz, left Misión San Juan Bautista to continue the exploration of the San Joaquín Valley started by Zalvidea and Ruíz. The party crossed the Coast Range northeasterly, proceeding up the east side of the valley and may have reached the Sacramento. Returning, the explorers continued down the east side of the valley and crossed the mountains to Misión San Fernando, attained on November 1. The party named the Merced and Mariposa rivers, and the Dolores (Tuolumne), Guadalupe (Stanislaus), and the Río de la Pasión (Calaveras).

September 3, 1808—Father Buenaventura Sitjar, cofounder of San Antonio, Soledad and San Miguel missions, died at San Antonio, his body being buried in the mission church. Sitjar was born in 1739 at Porrera, Mallorca. He became a Franciscan at Palma in 1758, reached Mexico in 1770, and California in the same year. A faithful and a studious missionary, he compiled an Indian vocabulary and a valuable report on suitable mission sites.

January 26, 1810—Father Marcelino Ciprés, co-

founder of Misión Santa Inés, died at Misión San
Miguel, where he was buried. Ciprés was a native of
Huesca, Aragon, Spain, took the Franciscan habit at
Saragossa, came to Mexico in 1793 and to California in
1795. He was attached to San Antonio and San Luís
Obispo. He learned the native language of the Indians
at San Antonio and evinced as much interest in the
material, as he did in the spiritual, welfare of his
charges.

January 14, 1811—Father Francisco Dumetz, one of
the founders of Misión San Fernando, died at San
Gabriel. Dumetz was a native of Mallorca, and arrived
in California, via Mexico, in 1771. He officiated at San
Diego, San Carlos, San Buenaventura, San Fernando,
and San Gabriel. He was buried at San Gabriel.
Though a competent missionary, he was one of the
least prominent among them. Dumetz was the last
survivor of the Franciscans who came early to California.

October 15, 1811—Fathers Ramón Abella of Misión
San Francisco, and Buenaventura Fortuni of San José,
started an expedition from the presidio of San Francisco that resulted in exploration by water of the lower
San Joaquín River, the first navigation of the Sacramento River, and the naming of San Pedro and San
Pablo points. They returned to the presidio on October 30.

September 10, 1812—Fort Ross was established by
Ivan A. Kuskof, Russian explorer, and named from the
root of the word Russia. Aleuts were employed in the
construction of the necessary buildings which Russia

hoped would prove the beginning of her dominion over the northwest coast of America.

December 8, 1812—"El Año de los Temblores" or "the Year of the Earthquakes," as it subsequently became known to the Spanish-Californians, started with a severe shock, felt from San Diego to La Purísima. In the first quake, the tower of Misión San Juan Capistrano fell, killing forty neophytes. At San Gabriel the church was badly cracked and the main altar fell. The second quake, on December 21, wrecked La Purísima, threw over a corner of Santa Inés, damaged the tower and façade of San Buenaventura, and cracked the walls at San Fernando. Little damage was done to ranchhouses.

July 24, 1814—Capt. José Dario Argüello, *comandante* of the presidio of Santa Barbara and ranking military officer in California, became ad interim governor upon the death of Don José Joaquín de Arrillaga at Soledad Mission. Arrillaga was born of noble parentage at Aya, Spain, in 1750, entered military service at Horcasitas, Sonora, in 1777, served in Texas in 1780-

1783, then came to Baja California as lieutenant-governor of the Californias. He served as ad interim governor on Romeu's death and, finally, at his death, had been for fourteen years governor. He was highly regarded by superiors, subordinates and the missionaries. He was buried at Soledad Mission.

December 23, 1814—Father Antonio Calzada, one of the founders of Misión Santa Inés, died at the mission, where his body was buried. Calzada was born in Florida, November 24, 1760, took the Franciscan habit in Havana in 1780, was ordained in Mexico in 1784, and came to California in 1787. Here he served at San Gabriel, La Purísima, and Santa Inés.

December 31, 1814—Lieut.-Col. Pablo Vicente Solá was appointed governor to succeed Capt. José Argüello who had functioned as acting governor since Arrillaga's death on July 24, 1814. Solá arrived at Monterey, August 30, 1815.

January 15, 1816—Thomas Doak, a sailor from the ship *Albatross,* landed at Refugio Rancho north of Santa Barbara, and became the first American settler in California. He was baptized at Misión San Carlos, December 22.

October 2, 1816—Otto von Kotzebue, commanding the *Rurik,* fitted out at the expense of the Russian Count Rumiantzof for an exploring voyage to the north Pacific, anchored in San Francisco Bay. The Russians entertained the Spanish-Californians, and in turn were entertained with numerous fiestas. Three books by members of the expedition describe California at greater or lesser length. Kotzebue wrote *A Voyage of*

Discovery into the South Sea, and Behring's Straits, published in London in 1821; Adelbert Von Chamisso, a naturalist member of the party, published his *Riese Um Die Welt* in Berlin in 1856, and Louis Choris, an artist, his *Voyage pittoresque autour du monde,* in Paris in 1822.

May 13, 1817—Lieut. Luís Argüello, *comandante* of the presidio of San Francisco, accompanied by Fathers Ramón Abella and Narciso Durán, pastors of the missions of San Francisco de Asís and San José, left San Francisco to explore, by water, the Sacramento and San Joaquín rivers. After proceeding up both rivers for a considerable distance, the party returned to San Francisco on May 26.

December 14, 1817—Misión San Rafael Arcángel was founded by Fathers Luís Gil y Taboada, Ramón Abella, Narciso Durán and Vicente Francisco Sarría—the twentieth Franciscan mission in California. It was named for Saint Raphael Archangel, "one of the seven who stand before the Lord."

November 20, 1818—Hypolyte Bouchard, commanding a French privateer carrying the revolutionary flag of Buenos Aires, with two frigates, the *Argentina* or *La Gentila,* and the *Santa Rosa* or *Libertad,* anchored in Monterey. Bouchard attacked the port on the 21st; landed and captured the town on the 22nd; and departed after looting it on the 26th.

December 2, 1818—Bouchard plundered Refugio Rancho near Dos Pueblos, or the present Naples, north of Santa Barbara.

December 6, 1818—Bouchard anchored at Santa

Barbara, arranged exchange of prisoners captured at Refugio Rancho, but did not attack the town. He sailed some time between December 9 and 12.

December 14, 1818—Bouchard landed at San Juan Capistrano for supplies, burned a few Indian huts and departed on the 15th or 16th, quitting California.

October 18, 1821—An expedition under command of Capt. Luís Argüello left the presidio of San Francisco on an exploration journey that eventually took them up the Sacramento Valley, possibly as far as the Willamette River, but probably only to Shasta or Weaverville, thence back via the Russian River and the present Napa and Sonoma counties. It was the most extensive northern expedition ever made by the Spanish by land in California. The party was back at San Francisco on November 15, 1821.

PART II

"LIBERTY, FRATERNITY, EQUALITY"
(1822–1846)

PART II

"LIBERTY, FRATERNITY, EQUALITY"

(1822–1846)

THE heels of the conquerors grew increasingly heavy on the necks of the Mexicans. The divine afflatus, once so virtuously flaunted, had given way to the greed of mercenaries. By slow attrition the spirit of a once-proud and regal people was bent to the wills and to the lashes of mighty masters. Serfdom was imposed upon the New World.

Out in California, far removed from conniving and oppressing viceroys, missions, presidios and pueblos thrived. Huge herds of cattle ranged over emerald hillsides and great ranchos sprawled in riotous pattern from San Diego to Sonoma. Here was peace; here was plenty; here was Arcady.

Then, with an amazing acceleration, the storm broke. The lash had fallen once too often on bleeding backs. Led by the parish priest, Miguel Hidalgo, carrying the banner of the Virgin of Guadalupe, a whole nation rallied in revolt. The rebellion flourished and succeeded, and there followed, first, the ephemeral empire of Agustín Iturbide, and then the republic under López de Santa Anna. The Spanish lion succumbed before the Mexican serpent.

The rapid transition from Spanish province to empire to republic ushered in three decades of insurgency in California. On the fringe of nowhere, removed from the restraining hands of the central government, intriguing *políticos* found the land a fertile one for their nefarious plots. The supplication of overburdened millions—"Liberty, fraternity, equality"—here became the deceitful shibboleth of oafs and knaves.

April 11, 1822—Gov. Pablo Vicente Solá, his officers, and the soldiers stationed at the presidio of Monterey replaced the Spanish flag with the standard of the new Mexican Empire and took an oath of allegiance to Emperor Iturbide. Soldiers at the presidios of Santa Barbara and San Francisco took the same oath on the 13th, and at San Diego on the 20th. Thus California ceased forever to be a province of Spain and became a part of the future Mexican republic.

May 21, 1822—California held its first general election at Monterey, when electors representing five presidial districts met and chose Gov. Pablo Vicente Solá as *diputado* to represent the province at the *córtes* of the Mexican Empire, to which California had pledged its allegiance on April 11.

September 26, 1822—Agustín Fernandez de San Vicente, representing the Mexican Emperor Iturbide, arrived at Monterey to proclaim California a province of independent Mexico and to establish a new local government.

November 9, 1822—The first *diputación* or provincial legislature in California was elected and installed at Monterey.

November 22, 1822—Capt. Luís Argüello was elected governor to succeed Pablo Vicente Solá, who became provincial *diputado* for California at the imperial *córtes* of Mexico. Solá was a native of Mondragon, Spain. He reached Monterey August 30, 1815, following his appointment as governor in March. His administration was occupied in combatting insurgency, and he seems to have been thoroughly dissatisfied with his position. His life after leaving California for Mexico is not known.

April 28, 1823—Father Mariano Payeras, sixth president of the California missions, died at Misión La Purísima Concepción.

July 4, 1823—Misión San Francisco Solano, twenty-first, and last, of the Franciscan missions established in Alta California, was founded by Father José Altimira. Located on the northern shore of San Francisco Bay, it was named for Saint Francis Solano (1549-1610), a Franciscan friar who served many years in South America.

August 24, 1823—Father José Señan, seventh president of the California missions, died at Misión San Buenaventura.

January 7, 1824—With the arrival of news of the downfall of the Mexican Empire dominated by Iturbide, and the creation of the Mexican republic, Spanish-Californians, unwilling at the moment to declare themselves in favor either of a central Federal government or a union of States, adopted a *"Plan de Gobierno"* for the government of the region. This created a general convention for the promulgation of laws, set salaries and duties of public officials, and concentrated judicial jurisdiction in justices of the peace, commanders of the presidios and, finally, in the governor—at that time Don Luís Antonio Argüello.

February 21, 1824—Indian neophytes of the central California missions initiated a revolt against the missionaries with an uprising at Misión Santa Inés and Misión La Purísima Concepción. The dissatisfaction spread to Misión Santa Barbara on February 22. Buildings were burned at Santa Inés and casualties included four whites and seven Indians killed at La Purísima; two Indians killed and four whites wounded at Santa Barbara, and three whites and sixteen Indians killed on March 16 at La Purísima.

August 18, 1824—The Mexican Congress adopted a colonization decree providing for colonization of lands in Mexico including California, promised security to foreigners, and withheld from colonization lands within twenty leagues of the boundaries of foreign nations or within ten leagues of the coast. Other clauses provided that lands colonized were to be tax-free for five years after publication of decree; Mexican citizens were to be given preference in selection of lands; lands were to be restricted to one square league (5,000 square varas) of irrigable land, four leagues of land dependent on rain, or six leagues of grazing lands; and that all holding land must reside in the republic.

October 8, 1824—Otto von Kotzebue, commanding the Russian frigate, *Predpriatie,* en route to protect the Russian company on the northwest coast, anchored in San Francisco Bay. This was his second visit to California.

January 31, 1825—Lieut.-Col. José María de Echeandía was appointed governor of California, new territory of the Republic of Mexico, to succeed Luís Antonio Argüello. Don Luís was California's first native governor. He was born at San Francisco June 21, 1784, his godparents being José Joaquín Moraga and wife.

He entered the military service at San Francisco in 1799, was promoted rapidly, participated in several exploration expeditions and became governor in 1822. Of him, his successor reported: "Courage, proved; ability, more than average; military conduct, indifferent; health, broken; loyalty, supposed faithful. His services merit all consideration, but his conduct is now loose, doubtless from excessive drinking." He died at San Francisco March 27, 1830, and was buried in the mission church next to Father Esténega.

March 26, 1825—California, through its *diputación*, ratified the constitution of "los Estados Unidos Mejicanos," adopted October 4, 1824, and thus became a territory of the new Republic of Mexico. The various presidios and pueblos of California individually ratified the constitution before the end of May, 1825.

November 3,. 1825—Father Estévan Tapis, founder of Misión Santa Inés, died at San Juan Bautista, and was buried in the church there. Tapis was born at Santa Coloma de Farnes, Catalonia, Spain, in 1754, taking the Franciscan habit at Gerona in 1778. He came to Mexico in 1786 and to California in 1790. Here he served successively at San Luís Obispo, Santa Barbara, San Carlos, La Purísima, Santa Inés, and San Juan Bautista. On Father Lasuén's death, Tapis officiated as president of the missions until 1812, subsequently becoming the bishop's vicar. He performed his duties ably and was popular with both the clergy and the military.

July 25, 1826—Secularization of the missions of California was started with the decree of Gov. José María de Echeandía, authorizing the Indians of the districts of San Diego, Santa Barbara, and Monterey to form pueblos and hold lands under strict supervision and severe regulation.

November 6, 1826—Capt. Frederick William Beechey, R.N., in H.M.S. *Blossom,* returning from an arctic expedition to Behring Straits, anchored in San Francisco Bay. Beechey mapped San Francisco Bay, gave names to a number of theretofore unnamed landmarks, touched at Monterey early in January, sailed for Hawaii January 5, returned to Monterey October 29, 1827, remained until December 17 when he again visited San Francisco, from which port he sailed January 3, 1828, for San Blas and England, via Cape Horn and Brazil. The chronicle of his journeys and his impressions of California are contained in his *Narrative of a Voyage to the Pacific and Beering's Strait,* published in London in 1831.

November 27, 1826—Traveling southwesterly from Bear River, Utah, along the general route of the present Arrowhead Trail, Jedediah Strong Smith, with a group of trappers, reached Misión San Gabriel—the first white man to arrive in California overland from the eastern United States.

January 27, 1827—Auguste Duhaut-Cilly, commanding the French ship *Le Héros,* arrived at San Francisco in the course of a trading voyage around the world. After trading up and down the California coast, Duhaut-Cilly sailed from San Pedro for Callao, Peru, October 20. He returned to Monterey May 3, 1828, again traversed the coast, and sailed for Hawaii from San Diego, August 30, 1828. Duhaut-Cilly recorded his observations about California in his book, *Voyage autour du monde, principalement a la Californie et aux Iles Sandwich,* published in Paris in 1834.

May 27, 1827—Jedediah Strong Smith with two companions began the ascent of the Sierra Nevadas, which took eight days, from a camp on the Merced River. These were the first white men to cross the Sierra. Smith went on to Salt Lake to a rendezvous with his partners in the fur trade, arriving about June 17.

July 13, 1827—The California *diputación,* or legislature, adopted and forwarded a proposal to the supreme government in Mexico that the name of the territory be changed to "Montezuma," and that Los Angeles be made the capital and re-named "Villa Victoria de la Reina de Los Angeles," to avoid confusing it with Puebla de Los Angeles in Mexico. No attention seems ever to have been paid to the matter in Mexico.

March 27, 1828—Sylvester Pattie and his son, James Ohio Pattie, with six companion trappers, arrived in San Diego under an order of arrest signed by Gov. José María de Echeandía, after they had made their way westward from Santa Fé to Misión Santa Catalina, in Baja California. The Patties spent two years in California, mostly in confinement, but their visit was notable in virtue of their observations, which the younger Pattie recorded under the title, *The Personal Narrative of James O. Pattie,* first published in Cin-

cinnati in 1831. They claim to have vaccinated twenty-two thousand Spanish-Californians for smallpox in 1829.

April 16, 1829—Henry Delano Fitch eloped with Josefa Carrillo, daughter of Joaquín Carrillo of San Diego, after priests at San Diego refused to marry them. In the *Vulture* they reached Valparaiso, where they were married July 3. On returning to California they were arrested, and after being brought before an ecclesiastical court at San Gabriel, presided over by Father José Sánchez, on charges that their marriage was unlawful, it was found by the court that though it was not legitimate, it was not null, but valid. Fitch was sentenced to present the pueblo church at Los Angeles with a bell of at least fifty pounds weight in view of "the great scandal which Don Enrique has caused in the province."

May 5, 1829—Alférez José Antonio Sánchez of San Francisco led an attack on Estanislao, native chief of the Cosumnes Indian tribe who, though baptized and educated at Misión San José, and once an *alcalde* or mayor there, had reverted and attacked the whites and the mission Indians in the San José and Santa Clara districts. Estanislao remained unconquered despite the fact that Sánchez' forces were augmented by troops under Alférez M. G. Vallejo.

November 12, 1829—Disaffected soldiers rebelled, seized Monterey, chose Joaquín Solís as leader, and revolted against the Mexican administration in California. San Juan, Santa Clara, San José and San Francisco joined the rebellion, as did San Miguel and Santa Inés. After attacking Santa Barbara, Solís fled on January 15, 1830. The revolt was broken when forces of Gov. José María de Echeandía recaptured Monterey on January 20, 1830.

March 8, 1830—Lieut.-Col. Manuel Victoria was made *jefe político,* or governor, of the territory of California to succeed José María de Echeandía. Prior to his appointment as governor, Echeandía had been a lieutenant-colonel of engineers in Mexico. During his administration he became the target for much undeserved criticism from Spanish-Californians. He served as ad interim governor after the abdication of Victoria in 1831, returned to Mexico in 1832, and died about 1860.

November 22, 1830—Father Magín Catalá, co-founder of Misión San Juan Bautista, died at Misión

Santa Clara, where his body was buried. Catalá was born at Montblanch, Catalonia, Spain, about 1761, and became a Franciscan at Barcelona in 1777. He arrived in Mexico in 1786 and in California in 1794. Though officiating at the founding of San Juan he served continuously as pastor of Santa Clara for thirty-seven years. Suffering constant illness, he was credited with prophetic powers. His exemplary and laborious life won him the devotion of all who knew him.

November 29, 1831—Pío Pico, Juan Bandini and José Antonio Carrillo led a revolt and seized the presidio of San Diego as a protest against the failure of Gov. Manuel Victoria to convoke the *diputación* and as a protest, too, against the exiling of Carrillo, Abel Stearns, et al. The rebels marched north, engaged in battle December 5 with Victoria and his soldiers near Cahuenga, one man being killed on each side, and Victoria severely wounded. Victoria was taken to San Gabriel, and on December 6 entered into negotiations which led to his abdication and the calling of the *diputación*.

December 9, 1831—José María de Echeandía assumed the office of ad interim governor of California, following the abdication of Manuel Victoria and pending the convocation of the *diputación*.

January 11, 1832—Pío Pico was chosen by a session of the *diputación* at Los Angeles to become *jefe político interino,* or ad interim governor, succeeding José María de Echeandía who had assumed the office December 9, 1831, on the abdication of Manuel Victoria. Echeandía later protested the action of the *diputación* as illegal and by February 16, Pico abandoned his claim to the office.

February 1, 1832—Agustín Zamorano, formerly secretary to Manuel Victoria, protested the assumption of office of governor by José María de Echeandía by the *pronunciamento de Monterey,* and proposed a joint rulership of California by military *comandantes*— Echeandía in the south and Zamorano in the north, until a governor could be legally appointed from Mexico. The plan was adopted and Echeandía and Zamorano thus ruled, but not as civil governors, until the appointment of José Figueroa, May 9, 1832, and his arrival at Monterey, January 14, 1833.

May 9, 1832—Gen. José Figueroa was appointed governor of California by President Carlos María Bustamante. Figueroa arrived in Monterey by boat from Acapúlco after many vicissitudes, January 14, 1833.

January 14, 1833—Ten missionaries from the college of Nuestra Señora de Guadalupe de Zacatecas (Franciscans) arrived at Monterey with Gov. José Figueroa, in charge of their prefect, Father Francisco García Diego y Moreno. Shortly thereafter they assumed charge of the seven missions from San Carlos northward. The Fernandino Franciscans, the original colonizers of California, retired to the southern missions. The new missionaries were known as Guadalupanos or Zacatecanos. Authorities agree that the Zacatecanos were lax morally, intellectually inferior to the Fernandinos, and inclined to be cruel to the Indians.

August 17, 1833—The original decree ordering the secularization of the missions of California, which involved the installation of civil administrators to handle temporal affairs and the dispersal of lands to Indian neophytes and others, was passed by the Congress of Mexico. Instructions as to procedure were issued by Gov. José Figueroa August 9, 1834. First mission secularized was San Diego. No date is given but it may have been in 1833, even before formal instructions were issued. It was followed by: Santa Cruz, August 24, 1834; San Francisco de Asís and Santa Barbara, September, 1834; San Carlos, 1834; San Francisco Solano, San Rafael and San Fernando, October, 1834; San Juan Capistrano, San Luís Rey, San Gabriel and La Purísima Concepción, November, 1834; San Juan Bautista, 1835; San Antonio, June, 1835; San Luís Obispo, October, 1835; San Miguel and San José, 1836; Santa Inés and San Buenaventura, June 23, 1836; and Santa Clara, 1837. No date is available for Soledad.

December 15, 1833—Father Luís Gil y Taboada, co-founder of Misión San Rafael, died at San Luís Obispo, where he was buried in the mission church. Gil y Taboada was born at Guanajuato, Mexico, in 1773, became a Franciscan at Querétaro in 1792, and came to California in 1801. Subsequently he was a missionary at San Francisco, San José, Santa Inés, Santa Barbara, San Gabriel, La Purísima, San Rafael, Santa Cruz, and San Luís Obispo. In 1814 he blessed the cornerstone of the Los Angeles church. He was skilled as a physician and surgeon, and is said to have delivered many children by Cæsarian section. Popular with his parishioners, he was at one time accused of undue familiarity with women. His superiors regarded him as innocent, though imprudent.

August 9, 1834—Gov. José Figueroa issued his famous *Reglamentto Provisional para la Secularización de las misiónes de la Alta California,* the first major piece of printing undertaken by California's first printer, Agustín Zamorano, providing for the conversion of missions into pueblos; friars to be relieved of temporal duties; each head of a family to be given a lot one hundred to four hundred *varas* square; *ejidos* to be assigned for pueblos; half of livestock, chattels, seeds, etc., to be distributed pro rata; government to be in the hands of *ayuntamientos;* mission libraries and church goods to remain in charge of priests.

September 1, 1834—A party of Mexican colonists, headed by José María Padrés and José María Hijar, totalling some two hundred and including nineteen farmers, eleven painters, twelve seamstresses, eight carpenters, eight tailors, five shoemakers, five tinners, five silversmiths, two hatters, two physicians, two barbers, two saddlers, two blacksmiths, two printers, two goldsmiths, one mathematician, one gardener, one surgeon, one machinist, one ribbon-maker, one rebozo-maker, one midwife, one distiller, one candy-maker, one vermicelli-maker, one navigator, one founder, one porkman, one musician, one vintner, one apothecary, one boatman, one carriage-maker, and six teachers, arrived at San Diego by sea from San Blas. The company was known as the *Compañia Cosmopolitana.* Legend has it that the *Natalia* the vessel on which the journey was made and which was wrecked at Monterey December 21, was the one on which Napoleon escaped from Elba in 1815.

May 23, 1835—Gen. Miguel Barragan issued a decree raising the pueblo of Los Angeles to the status of a "city," and making it the capital of California.

May 24, 1835—Father Vicente Francisco Sarría, founder of Misión San Rafael, died on the altar during services at Soledad Mission. He was buried in the church at San Antonio. Sarría was born in 1767 at San Estévan de Echabarris, in Bilbao, Spain. There he became a Franciscan in 1783. He journeyed to Mexico in 1805 and to California in 1809. Here he served at San Carlos and Soledad. Between 1813-1819 and 1823-1830 he held the position of *comisario-prefecto* of the province. He was also president of the missions from 1823 to 1825. A scholar, able executive, tolerant, and yet devoutly religious, Sarría was a worthy successor to Serra and Lasuén. He wrote extensively and well on mission subjects.

June 24, 1835—Gov. José Figueroa ordered Alférez

M. G. Vallejo to found a "garrison, town and colony" on the northern frontier to protect it against invasion by Russians or other foreigners. Vallejo chose the site of Misión San Francisco Solano, of which he had been previously made secular administrator, and named it Sonoma, an Indian word meaning "Valley of the Moon."

October 8, 1835—José Castro, chosen by José Figueroa, became *jefe político,* or governor, following the death of Figueroa on September 29, 1835. Figueroa's early life is obscure. Prior to his appointment as governor, he had been from 1824 on, *comandante-general* of Sonora. Undoubtedly he was California's best Mexican governor. He died of apoplexy and was buried in the mission church at Santa Barbara.

December 16, 1835—Col. Mariano Chico was appointed governor of California by President Miguel Barragan even before the death of José Figueroa was known in Mexico. Chico arrived at Santa Barbara "after the middle of April, 1836." In the interim both José Castro and Lieut.-Col. Nicolás Gutiérrez had acted as governor.

January 2, 1836—Lieut.-Col. Nicolás Gutiérrez who, since the death of José Figueroa, had been acting as military commander of California with José Castro as civil governor, took over Castro's office and title.

April 7, 1836—California's first vigilance committee executed, by hanging, Gervasio Alipas and María del Rosario Villa at Los Angeles for the murder of Domingo Felix, María's husband, on the road between

Los Angeles and San Gabriel. The vigilance committee was formed in John Temple's home, was headed by Victor Prudon, and was supported, under the name of "*Junta Defensora de la Seguridad Pública,*" by fifty prominent Angelinos.

September 6, 1836—Nicolás Gutiérrez reassumed the governorship of California following the flight of Col. Mariano Chico to Mexico in July. As Figueroa was California's best Mexican governor, Chico was its worst. Though a man of some ability, his morals and his habits invoked the enmity of the Spanish-Californians, who universally disliked him. He suffered, too, from a hostile *disputación.*

November 3, 1836—Don Juan Bautista Alvarado and José Castro, with one hundred Spanish-Californians, led a revolt against Gov. Nicolás Gutiérrez at Monterey, instigated by opposition to the Mexican practice of sending Mexicans to rule California, when many Californian leaders were available. Monterey capitulated and Gutiérrez surrendered November 5, fleeing to Cape San Lucas. Castro occupied the office of *comandante-general* until November 29, being succeeded by Alvarado as governor.

November 8, 1836—The territorial *disputación,* or assembly, of California adopted a declaration of independence from Mexico. The territory, it was declared, was to be known as "the free and sovereign State of California." The partition, which was engineered by Gov. Juan B. Alvarado, existed until July 9, 1837 when, after the election of Gen. Anastasio Bustamante as constitutional president of Mexico, Alvarado performed a *volte face* and again brought California back into the republic as a "department." The opposition of Los Angeles and other Southern California communities to the independent State doubtless influenced him in his course.

December 7, 1836—Juan B. Alvarado was declared governor of California by the *diputación,* succeeding José Castro who, as president of the *diputación,* had served since the surrender of Nicolás Gutiérrez on November 5, as both governor and *comandante-general.* M. G. Vallejo had succeeded Castro to the latter office on November 29.

December 30, 1836—A Mexican Federal decree was issued dividing the Californias into three districts, one extending virtually the length of the peninsula of Baja California; the second from Santo Domingo to El Buchón, and the third from San Luís Obispo to the Sonoma frontier. These, in turn, were divided into *partidos.* The northernmost district was divided at Llagas Creek, the head towns being San Juan de Castro and San Francisco Mission. The second district was divided between San Fernando and Cahuenga, and head towns were located at Los Angeles and Santa Barbara. The third district in Baja California was not divided at this time.

June 6, 1837—Don Carlos Carrillo was appointed provisional governor of the Department of the Californias by President Bustamante. He was inaugurated at Los Angeles, December 6, 1837, but Juan B. Alvarado consistently refused to recognize the appointment. Carrillo was removed in 1838.

October 18, 1837—Capt. Abel du Petit-Thouars, commanding the French Frigate *Vénus,* engaged in investigating the whale fisheries of the North Pacific, arrived at Monterey. He and his crew were welcomed and feted by Alvarado and his aides. The French visitor's observations were mainly scientific, but he did gather and translate several original documents, publishing them in his *Voyage autour du monde sur la Frégate La Vénus,* which was issued in Paris in 1840. His comments about the Spanish-Californians were restrained but favorable.

October 19, 1837—Capt. Sir Edward Belcher, R.N., commanding H.M.S. *Sulphur* and H.M.S. *Starling,* an English explorer making hydrographic surveys of the western coast and islands of California, arrived at San Francisco. What Belcher saw in, and thought about, California he detailed in his book, *Narrative of a Voyage Around the World,* published in London in 1843. Belcher succeeded to the command of the expedition at Panamá upon the illness of Capt. Beechey. Belcher entered San Francisco Bay for exploration purposes, but left California in December. He returned, arriving at Bodega Bay, September 20, 1839, moved leisurely down the coast, and finally quit California October 22. Belcher thought the Spanish-Californians were bandits and the region most repellent.

April 15, 1839—Abandonment of Fort Ross by the Russian American Company and the withdrawal of Russians from California was sanctioned by the Russian imperial government. Subsequently, on December 13, 1841, the company sold all the property at

Fort Ross and Bodega to John Sutter. The last of the Russians left Fort Ross in January, 1842.

July 1, 1839—John Augustus Sutter, destined to be the founder of Nueva Helvecia and California's most celebrated emigrant, arrived in San Francisco from Honolulu.

October 21, 1839—Capt. Cyrille Pierre Théodore Laplace, commanding the frigate *Artémise,* engaged in a hydrographic survey of the northwestern coast of America in the course of a voyage around the world, arrived at San Francisco. Laplace visited Bodega Bay, San Francisco, Santa Cruz, and Monterey, eventually leaving California on September 10. Laplace in his *Campagne de Circumnavigation de la frégate l'Artémise,* published in Paris in 1841, wrote of California in most complimentary terms.

March 10, 1840—The first Supreme Court of California, or *"Tribunal de Justicia,"* was formed by the *junta departamental,* acting under authority of the law of May 23, 1837. Judges or *minístros* were: Juan

Malarín, J. A. Carrillo, J. A. Estudillo, and A. M. Osio, with Juan Bandini as *fiscal* and Mariano Bonilla as secretary.

April 7, 1840—Isaac Graham, American trapper who had settled in California, was arrested by order of Gov. Juan B. Alvarado, at Natividad, on a charge of leading a revolt of foreigners against the Mexican government. By the 11th, thirty-eight other foreigners had been arrested. Later all other foreigners who had entered California illegally and who were not married to native women were arrested. On April 24 the prisoners sailed from Monterey on the *Joven Guipuzcoana,* stopping at Santa Barbara for other prisoners, destined for San Blas and the custody of the central government. A total of forty-seven were imprisoned at Tepic. On September 23, about twenty of the prisoners were ordered released, but Graham and the balance of the group did not gain their freedom until June, 1841. They were adjudged not guilty, were paid reparations approximating $250 each, were given *cartas de seguridad,* and returned to Monterey, where they arrived in July, 1841. Later additional reparations totalling $24,050 were paid to the exiles.

September 1, 1840—John Augustus Sutter was authorized by Gov. Juan B. Alvarado to erect what was later to be known as "Sutter's Fort" on the site of the present city of Sacramento. This marked the beginning of Sutter's reign over what he called "New Helvetia." He was empowered to pursue and capture robbers and unlicensed hunters, but not to wage war on the natives or others without specific authority. Sutter was born of

Swiss parentage in the Grand Duchy of Baden in 1803, emigrated to New York in 1834, moved to Missouri where he lived a few years; made his way to Oregon, thence to Hawaii, and finally reached San Francisco in July, 1839. On August 28, 1840, he was naturalized. His original land grant of eleven leagues was augmented in 1841 by the purchase of the property of the Russian colony at Fort Ross. By 1845 he was landed lord of the northern frontier. New Helvetia subsequently became the first stop of emigrants to California. The discovery of gold at his mill at Coloma in 1848 proved his undoing, for he was victimized by the ever-increasing horde of Argonauts. Poverty-stricken, the Legislature voted him a pension of $250 a month in 1864 and stopped it in 1878. Sutter went east in 1865 and conducted a fruitless campaign in Congress to secure redress for being deprived of his lands. He died in Washington, D. C., in 1880.

October 4, 1840—Father García Diego y Moreno, who came to California as prefect of the Zacatecan friars on January 14, 1833, while in Mexico was consecrated first bishop of the diocese of the Californias, the creation of which had been authorized on September 19, 1836. Diego y Moreno arrived in San Diego on the *Rosalind,* December 11, 1841. The bishop arrived at Santa Barbara on January 11, 1842, choosing it as the site of his see. On March 24, 1842, he consecrated the *hospicio* of Santa Barbara as California's first cathedral.

May 12, 1841—M. Eugène Duflot de Mofras, French emissary dispatched to Cailfornia to investigate the possibility of developing trade between France and Mexico and its colonies, arrived in Monterey on the *Ninfa*. Mofras visited every mission and settlement in California, and in 1844 published in French in Paris a three-volume (2 vol. and atlas) description of Upper and Lower California and Oregon, which has been

widely quoted. It was published under the title, *Exploration du Territoire de l'Oregon, des Californies, et de la Mer Vermeille*. Mofras' work provides an extensive description of the country at the time of his visit and exhibits a judicial attitude toward obtaining affairs.

June 18, 1841—Gov. Juan B. Alvarado granted eleven square leagues of land, comprising New Helvetia, to John Sutter.

August 14, 1841—The first exploring expedition sent to California by the United States, comprising six vessels and six hundred men, including many scientists, and commanded by Lieut. Charles Wilkes, anchored in San Francisco Bay. Wilkes' reports are contained in his *Narrative of the United States Exploring Expedition*

During the Years 1838-1842. The reports were mainly scientific in character.

November 4, 1841—The first overland emigrant train to California from mid-western United States, consisting of thirty-two men, one woman and one child, under the leadership of Capt. John Bartleson, arrived at John Marsh's ranch, Los Médanos. Included in the party were John Bidwell, Josiah Belden and others, who were destined to become celebrated California citizens.

November 10, 1841—An emigrant party of twenty-three men from New Mexico, under the leadership of John Rowland and William Workman, arrived at San Gabriel Mission.

January 1, 1842—The Russian colony at Fort Ross was formally abandoned. Lands and buildings were purchased by John Sutter in complicated negotiations, whereby the Russians ceded their property to the Mexican government, and the latter assumed and guaranteed Sutter's debt. This marked the end of the Russian attempt to gain California.

January 22, 1842—Gen. Manuel Micheltorena was appointed by President Antonio López de Santa Anna, "governor, *comandante-general* and inspector" of California. He took with him from Mexico an army consisting of one hundred and fifty pardoned convicts and one hundred regular soldiers, which the Californians promptly characterized as *"cholos,"* and arrived at San Diego August 25. He became civil governor on December 31, 1842, though he had taken office as military commander somewhat earlier. Depredations of the *cholos,* who stole from the Californios, created hostility and finally resulted in a revolt against Micheltorena, starting November 14, 1844, and forcing him to leave the region ultimately, with two hundred soldiers, from Monterey, March 26, 1845. Micheltorena succeeded Juan B. Alvarado, California's second native governor. Alvarado was born at Monterey, February 14, 1809, served as secretary of the *diputación,* 1827-1834, was a member of that body in 1835-1836, and president in the latter year. After his term as governor ended, he participated in the revolt successfully led by Pío Pico, became administrator of the Monterey custom-house, and received numerous large land grants, including Rancho Mariposas. He died July 13, 1882. His character embraced both good and bad elements. Historians rate him as shrewd but patriotic; honest but inclined to profligacy; and discount the prejudiced charges that he looted the missions for his own gain.

February 8, 1842—By a Mexican governmental decree of this date, administration of the large and long-established "Pious Fund," created by contributions from the religious rich for the support of missionary work among the barbarians of Sonora and the Californias, was taken away from church authorities and vested in civil government officials. Spoliation of the fund followed for many years, with constant controversy and litigation.

March 6, 1842—Father Lorenzo Quijas was appointed vice-prefect and Antonio Anzar, president, of the Zacatecan friars in charge of the northern missions of California.

March 9, 1842—The first discovery of placer gold in commercial quantities in California was made by Francisco López, majordomo of Misión San Gabriel, in Placerita Canyon, eight miles west of Newhall.

March 24, 1842—Bishop García Diego y Moreno, California's first bishop, consecrated the *hospicio* at Santa Barbara as California's first cathedral.

May 24, 1842—Father Ramón Abella, co-founder of Misión San Rafael, died at Santa Inés, where he was buried in the mission church. Abella was born at Monforte, Aragon, Spain, in 1764, became a Franciscan at Saragossa in 1784. He came to Mexico in 1795, and to California in 1798. He labored at San Francisco, San Carlos, San Luís Obispo and La Purísima. He was classed by his superiors as a most competent and zealous missionary, though somewhat weak in temporal management.

October 19, 1842—Under the erroneous impression that the United States and Mexico were at war, Com. Thomas Ap. Catesby Jones, commander of the United States Pacific Squadron, took possession of Monterey, hoisting the American flag over the *castillo*. The Californians signed articles of capitulation without a struggle. Two days later, upon discovering that he had been misinformed about the war and the suspected cession of California to England, Com. Jones took down the American flag, restored the town to the Californians, fired a salute to the Mexcian flag, and sent a message of apology to Gen. Manuel Micheltorena at Santa Barbara, who was then on his way north from Mexico to assume the governorship.

November 22, 1842—The first commercial shipment of gold was made by Abel Stearns to Alfred Robinson. It consisted of twenty ounces of California placer gold, to be forwarded to the mint in Philadelphia. This was taken from the placers discovered in Placerita Canyon, near Newhall.

March 29, 1843—Gov. Manuel Micheltorena restored temporal management of twelve missions—San Diego, San Luís Rey, San Juan Capistrano, San Gabriel, San Fernando, San Buenaventura, Santa Barbara, La Purísima, Santa Inés, Santa Clara, San Antonio and San José—to the California friars, on condition that one-eighth of the total annual produce of every description should be paid into the public treasury.

May 1, 1843—Thomas Oliver Larkin was appointed United States Consul "for the Port of Monterey, in California, and such other ports as shall be nearer thereto than to the residence of any other consul or vice-consul of the United States within the same allegiance." Larkin entered upon his duties April 2, 1844, and served until June 23, 1846. He was the only United States Consul ever to serve in California.

March 8, 1844—Capt. John Charles Frémont reached Sutter's Fort on his first overland exploration expedition from the Missouri River to California, via the south fork of the Platte River, South Pass, Fort Hall, Fort Boise, The Dalles, Klamath Lake, Carson River and Johnson Pass.

May 7, 1844—The first Catholic seminary in California, known as "Colegio Seminario de María Santísima de Guadalupe de Santa Inés de Californias," was founded at Santa Inés Mission. Father José Joaquín Jimeno was rector, and the first five students were José de los Santos Avila, Alejo Salmón, Agapito Cabrera, Ramón Gonzalez and Diego Villa.

November 14, 1844—Californians, angered at the depredations of Gov. Manuel Micheltorena's convict army, sent to govern them in 1842, started a revolt which resulted in Micheltorena leaving the country from San Pedro, March 12, 1845, and Monterey, March 26, after the bloodless battle of Cahuenga February 20, 1845, and the signing of the treaty of peace at San Fernando February 22, 1845, the treaty including his abdication.

December 13, 1844—The Elisha Stevens party of overland emigrants from the Missouri River—the first party to cross the Sierra via the later popular Truckee River and Donner Lake route, and the first party to bring a wagon-train into the central valleys of California—reached Sutter's Fort. The party consisted of some fifty men, women and children, and twelve wagons.

February 22, 1845—On the defeat of Manuel Micheltorena by Spanish-Californian insurgents, Don Pío Pico succeeded him as ad interim governor, and moved the capital to Los Angeles. On April 18, 1846, he was confirmed in office by the central government and held the position until the American conquest was terminated with the signing of the Capitulation of Cahuenga. Thus he became the State's third native, and its last Mexican, governor. Pico was born at San Gabriel in 1801, entered politics as a *vocal* in the *diputación* in 1828. Thenceforth he was active in State affairs, being chosen by the *diputación,* January 11, 1832, to succeed Echeandía as governor. Opposition being great, he abandoned his claims to the office. He was granted, at one time or another, Rancho Temecula and Santa Margarita y Las Flores. His final administration was sullied by the antedating of some land grants, and he was criticized for his handling of mission property. He fled to Mexico at the time of the American conquest, returning in 1848 to California, where he died September 11, 1894.

July 10, 1845—The Mexican Minister of Interior Relations ordered Gov. Pío Pico to prevent further immigration of Americans to California in view of increasingly strained relations between Mexico and the United States over the revolt of Texas from the Mexican Republic.

September 16, 1845—President James K. Polk appointed John Slidell of New Orleans secret agent to Mexico to negotiate the definition of a permanent boundary between the United States and Mexico, through the purchase of Upper California and New Mexico.

October 17, 1845—Secretary of State James Buchanan secretly instructed United States Consul Thomas O. Larkin to encourage the Spanish-Californians to resist French and English overtures, and intimated that should California decide to declare her independence from Mexico that the United States would render her its "kind offices."

October 28, 1845—Gov. Pío Pico issued a decree leasing or selling the following missions: San Juan Capistrano, sold to Juan Forster and James McKinley for $710; La Purísima Concepción, sold to John Temple for $1,110; San Luís Obispo, sold to Scott, Wilson and McKinley for $510; Santa Barbara, leased to Nicholas A. Den and Daniel Hill for $1,200 a year; San Buenaventura, leased to José Arnaz and Narciso Botello for $1,630 a year; Santa Inés, leased to José María Covarrubias and Joaquín Carrillo for $580 a year; San Fernando, leased to Andrés Pico and Juan Manso for $1,120 a year.

December 12, 1845—Capt. John Charles Frémont arrived at Sutter's Fort on his second exploration expedition to California and the Far West.

March 6, 1846—Capt. John C. Frémont erected a fort and raised the American flag on Gavilán Peak, preparing to resist orders of Gen. José Castro, requiring him and his men to leave California. Frémont remained here only three days, retreating on the night of March 9 to Sutter's Fort.

PART III

"MANIFEST DESTINY"
(1846–1848)

"MANIFEST DESTINY"

(1846–1848)

THE covetous eyes of England, of Russia, and of France inevitably settled upon the northwest coast of America. The "exploring" expeditions of La Pérouse, of Vancouver, of Kotzebue, ostensibly conducted in the sweet and unselfish cause of science, had carried the tales of California's fruitful valleys into distant courts, scheming lustfully for the extension of their dominions.

But, in the nature of things, it was decreed otherwise. Geographically and economically California belonged to the ambitious young republic reared under the Stars and Stripes. The United States were the one vigorous nation in a decadent world.

The flag follows trade—invariably. Shrewd Yankee merchants were assaulting Mexico's feeble northern salient by land and by sea. Their ammunition was crockery and tools, furniture and textiles, fripperies and fol-de-rols.

Overland, huge caravans penetrated the salient from the east. Into the Pacific and on to California came the brigs of the Boston men. They introduced among the New Mexicans and the Spanish-Californians the ways and the devices of their neighbors to the east. When the United States at long last determined to move their western frontier to the Pacific, the conquest was a mere formality. Fair, ruddy folk long before had captured the hearts and the allegiance of those in the new lands. That was "manifest destiny."

May 13, 1846—President James K. Polk proclaimed that "by the act of the Republic of Mexico a state of war exists between that government and the United States," thus initiating the hostilities that were shortly to result in the American conquest of California.

June 1, 1846—Father Narciso Durán, co-founder of Misión San Rafael, died at Santa Barbara, where he was buried in the mission church. Durán was born in 1776 at Castellon de Ampurias, Catalonia, Spain, took the Franciscan habit at Gerona in 1792, came to Mexico in 1803, and to California in 1806. Here he served at San José and Santa Barbara. Durán was president of the missions 1825-1827, 1831-1838, and 1844-1846. A high-minded and zealous priest, Durán likewise was an able and energetic administrator, managing mission affairs through the troublous times of secularization with marked ability. He wrote widely and capably, moreover, about the California establishments.

June 3, 1846—Secretary of War William L. Marcy ordered Col. Stephen W. Kearny to advance from Santa Fé and take possession of Upper California as commander-in-chief of all military and naval forces of the United States on the Pacific Slope.

June 14, 1846—Col. M. G. Vallejo, Lieut.-Col. Victor Prudon and Capt. Salvador Vallejo were seized and the Sonoma garrison was captured by American settlers, including Ezekiel Merritt, William B. Ide, Robert Semple and thirty others, as a preliminary move in the Bear Flag revolt. The prisoners were first transported to Capt. John C. Frémont's camp on the American River, and on June 16 or 17 were incarcerated, with Jacob P. Leese, who had acted as interpreter, at Sutter's Fort.

June 14, 1846—The Bear flag, standard of "The California Republic," was raised over the Plaza at Sonoma following the capture of Col. M. G. Vallejo, Lieut.-Col. Victor Prudon and Capt. Salvador Vallejo. A proclamation, issued on the 15th by William B. Ide, leader of the republican movement, charged that the citizens had been oppressed and deceived by the Mexican authorities, had been denied promised lands, and a fair and just government, and urged all peaceable and honest citizens to support the republic. Leaders in the revolt were Ide, Ezekiel Merritt, John Grigsby, Robert Semple, H. L. Ford, William Todd, Thomas Fallon, William Knight, William Hargrave, Samuel Kelsey, G. P. Swift, Samuel Gibson, and others.

July 5, 1846—Capt. John C. Frémont at Sonoma assumed command over the insurgent band which, under the leadership of William B. Ide, on June 14, 1846, had inaugurated the Bear Flag revolt. In a statement by Frémont, California was declared independent of Mexico and under martial law. The reorganized insurgents, together with Frémont's explorers, totalling two hundred and fifty, formed into what was known as the "California Battalion."

July 7, 1846—Capt. William Mervine, commander of the U.S.S. *Cyane* and U.S.S. *Savannah,* acting under orders from Com. John D. Sloat, raised the American flag over the custom-house at Monterey, thus formally taking possession of California for the United States. The occupation was achieved without a shot being fired.

July 9, 1846—Capt. John B. Montgomery, commanding the U.S.S. *Portsmouth,* raised the American flag in the public square at Yerba Buena, during the progress of the conquest of California by United States forces.

July 9, 1846—Lieut. Joseph Warren Revere, of the U.S.S. *Cyane,* on orders from Com. Sloat, hoisted the American flag at Sonoma, and took possession for the United States. The flag was raised on the staff in front of the barracks, until then occupied by the singular Bear Flag. Thus passed into oblivion the standard, and the "Republic," of California.

July 11, 1846—Capt. John C. Frémont or Lieut. Edward Kern (the record is not clear) raised the American flag over Sutter's Fort, under instructions received from Lieut. Joseph Warren Revere.

July 16, 1846—Capt. Thomas Fallon, patriotic United States citizen and a participant in the Bear Flag revolt, hoisted the American flag over the *juzgado,* or court, in San José with permission of Capt. John B. Montgomery, during the formal American conquest of California.

July 17, 1846—The American flag was raised over the pueblo of San Juan Bautista by Capt. Daingerfield Fauntleroy of the U.S.S. *Savannah,* in command of a company of volunteer dragoons delegated to maintain order and hold possession of the region about Monterey for the United States.

July 23, 1846—Com. Robert F. Stockton replaced Com. John D. Sloat as "commander-in-chief of all forces and operations on land," during the American conquest of California. On July 29, 1846, Stockton succeeded Sloat as commander of the United States Pacific Squadron.

July 29, 1846—Capt. John C. Frémont landed at San Diego from the U.S.S. *Cyane,* raised the American flag, and took possession of the pueblo for the United States.

July 31, 1846—Mormon colonists numbering two

hundred and thirty, under the leadership of Elder Samuel Brannan, arrived in San Francisco after a voyage on the *Brooklyn* from New York via Cape Horn and Honolulu.

August 4, 1846—Com. Robert F. Stockton took possession of the presidio and pueblo of Santa Barbara by raising the Stars and Stripes.

August 6, 1846—The Stars and Stripes was raised and possession was taken of San Pedro for the United States by Com. Robert F. Stockton.

August 13, 1846—United States forces under command of Com. Robert F. Stockton and Maj. John C. Frémont, seized Los Angeles for the United States and hoisted the Stars and Stripes.

August 15, 1846—*The Californian,* first newspaper to be published in California, owned by Robert Semple and Walter Colton, made its initial appearance as a weekly at Monterey.

September 2, 1846—Com. Robert F. Stockton appointed Maj. John C. Frémont as military commandant, or governor, of the "territory" of California.

September 4, 1846—Alcalde Walter Colton impaneled at Monterey the first jury ever called to try a legal action in California.

September 23, 1846—Californian insurgents under the leadership of Sérbulo Varela initiated a revolt against United States occupation by attacking the garrison of American soldiers at Los Angeles under command of Lieut. Archibald H. Gillespie. Shortly thereafter this developed into a general insurrection led by Capt. José María Flores, and participated in by three hundred Californians. During the hostilities there was fought the battle of Chino Rancho (September 26-27), won by the Californians, who subsequently attacked Los Angeles again and forced Gillespie and his men to retreat to San Pedro and take refuge on the U.S.S. *Vandalia.*

September 26, 1846—The first battle between United States forces and Californians during the American conquest occurred at the Chino Rancho of Isaac Williams. The Californians, under José del Carmen Lugo, Sérbulo Varela, et al., were victorious. One Califorian was killed, and three Californians and three Americans were wounded, and fifteen Americans were captured. This contest was a part of the Flores revolt, initiated on September 23, 1846.

September 28, 1846—John Brown, known as "Juan Flaco" or "Long John," an American soldier, arrived in San Francisco after having made the fastest horseback ride ever recorded from Los Angeles. Brown carried a message asking aid from Com. Robert F. Stockton for American military forces besieged by Spanish-Californians in Los Angeles. Brown left Los Angeles at

8 P.M. September 24, reached Santa Barbara at 11 P.M. September 25, Monterey on September 27, and San Francisco at 8 P.M. on September 28. He had traversed six hundred and thirty miles in four days.

October 8, 1846—American sailors under Capt. William Mervine attacked Californian insurgents under command of Capt. José María Flores at the battle of Dominguez Rancho. Six sailors were killed and six wounded in the skirmish. The dead were buried at Isla de los Muertos, or "Deadman's Island," in San Pedro Bay, which gave the location its name.

October 31, 1846—The Donner overland emigrant party, destined for California and entrapped by snows in the Sierra Nevada, was forced to establish camp in the vicinity of modern Truckee and Donner Lake. Before being rescued by four relief expeditions sent out from Sutter's Fort, thirty-nine members of the party of eighty-seven died from illness, cold and starvation. The last survivor in the most appalling of all emigrant-train tragedies was not rescued until April 17, 1847.

November 16, 1846—American forces under Capt. Charles Burroughs, of Frémont's California Battalion, and Californians under Comandante Manuel Castro, engaged in battle at Natividad, near San Juan Bautista. American casualties amounted to some four or five killed and five or six wounded. The losses of the Californians were about the same. The victory was an American one.

December 6, 1846—Eighty Californians under Capt. Andrés Pico, and one hundred and sixty United States soldiers under command of Gen. Stephen W. Kearny, plus forty more United States troops under command of Capt. Archibald H. Gillespie, engaged in the battle of San Pascual, between Warner's Ranch and San Diego. Eighteen United States soldiers were killed and nineteen wounded. None among the Californians was killed, but twelve were wounded. At the end of hostilities United States troops held the battleground, technically victorious.

January 8, 1847—The battle of San Gabriel was fought at Paso de Bartolo on the San Gabriel River, just north of the present town of Whittier, by California forces under Com. José María Flores and Americans under Com. Robert F. Stockton and Gen. Stephen W. Kearny. The Americans were victorious after a two-hour engagement, casualties being two dead and eight wounded. Casualties among the California forces were the same.

January 9, 1847—The first issue of the first newspaper in San Francisco and the second newspaper in California, the *California Star,* appeared in San Francisco. It was published by Samuel Brannan, and E. P. Jones was its first editor.

January 9, 1847—California forces under Com. José María Flores and American soldiers under Com. Robert F. Stockton and Gen. Stephen W. Kearny, engaged in the battle of La Mesa in southeastern Los Angeles, the last engagement of the American conquest. Casualties were one killed and an unknown number wounded on the Californians' side, and five wounded on the Americans' side.

January 10, 1847—American forces under Com. Robert F. Stockton and Gen. Stephen W. Kearny re-conquered Los Angeles and raised the American flag, which had been removed with the advent of the revolt of Com. José María Flores.

January 13, 1847—Gen. Andrés Pico and Lieut.-Col. John C. Frémont signed articles of capitulation at

Rancho Cahuenga, thus terminating all hostilities between Californians and American forces.

January 19, 1847—Lieut.-Col. John C. Frémont assumed the office of first American civil governor of California, following his appointment to the post by Com. Robert F. Stockton under date of January 16, 1847.

January 29, 1847—Three hundred and forty volunteer soldiers of the Mormon Battalion, mustered into military service July 16, 1846, to aid the operations of the Army of the West, under command of Lieut.-Col. Philip St. George Cooke, arrived at San Diego. After garrisoning San Diego, San Luís Rey, and occupying Los Angeles, the battalion was mustered out at Los Angeles July 16, 1847. The bulk of the volunteers returned to Salt Lake City.

March 1, 1847—Lieut.-Col. John C. Frémont was deposed as the first American civil governor of California after serving but forty days, by Gen. Stephen W. Kearny, who assumed the office on instructions from the President of the United States.

March 6, 1847—The first detachment of the First New York Volunteers, recruited in New York as a part of Gen. Stephen W. Kearny's Army of the West, and mustered in at Governor's Island August 1, 1846, arrived at San Francisco under command of Col. Jonathan D. Stevenson. The regiment journeyed to California around Cape Horn in five small transports. Hostilities being at an end on their arrival, the soldiers were employed in garrisoning San Francisco, Monterey, Santa Barbara, La Paz, in Baja California, and elsewhere. The regiment was ordered mustered out of service on August 7, 1848, many of the soldiers taking up permanent residence in California.

April 15, 1847—N. P. Trist, appointed commissioner to Mexico, received instructions to negotiate for the cession of the two Californias, New Mexico, and the privilege of a right-of-way across the Isthmus of Tehuantepec for $30,000,000, or $20,000,000 for New Mexico and Upper California. He was recalled by Secretary of State James Buchanan, on October 4, 1847, but remained to negotiate peace terms.

May 16, 1847—Though Protestant services had been held in California in 1579 by Sir Francis Drake, and revived to some degree by Rev. William Roberts, a missionary from Oregon in 1846, the first formal services in American California seem to have been held on this date at San Francisco by Rev. James H. Wilber of the Oregon Methodist Mission.

May 31, 1847—Gen. Stephen W. Kearny, governor of California, placed Col. Richard B. Mason of the First United States Dragoons in charge of all military forces in the territory, and appointed him acting governor pending Kearny's journey to Washington.

July 4, 1847—Fort Moore in Los Angeles, designed to accommodate two hundred soldiers and furnish protection to the little pueblo, was dedicated as the city held its first American Independence Day celebration. The fort was named for Capt. Benjamin D. Moore of the First United States Dragoons, who was killed at the battle of San Pascual. It was abandoned in 1848.

August 22, 1847—Lieut.-Col. John C. Frémont was placed under arrest at Fort Leavenworth by Gen. Stephen W. Kearny and ordered to report to the adjutant-general at Washington to face charges of insubordination. Frémont's court-martial started on September 27 and lasted until January 11, 1848. He was found guilty on January 31 and sentenced to dismissal from the army. On a recommendation of clemency by seven members of the court, President Polk, though approving the sentence, remitted the penalty and ordered Frémont to resume his sword. Frémont declined to avail himself of clemency, however, and sent in his resignation, which was accepted on March 14, 1848. Frémont had been active in Western exploration and military affairs since 1842. He was born in Georgia, became a lieutenant of topographical engineers in 1838, married Jessie Benton, daughter of Senator Thomas H. Benton (thus becoming his protégé) in 1841; reached the Rockies on his first exploring expedition in 1842, and California, during his second and third, in 1844 and 1845. He clashed frequently with the Spanish-Californians, and participated without authority in the

Bear Flag Revolt in 1846. Stockton appointed him governor January 19, 1847, and Kearny deposed him March 1, assuming the office himself. After his court-martial, Frémont served as United States Senator from California in 1850-1851, and in 1856 was nominated for the Presidency by the Republicans, but was defeated by Buchanan. In 1878 he became governor of the Territory of Arizona for a brief term. He died July 13, 1890, in New York City. Frémont has been greatly maligned and just as strongly defended. He was, in brief, a fairly intelligent and courageous man, of only moderate ability, and an adventurer who operated under an ægis of particularly good fortune.

November 15, 1847—The first steamship in California waters, the *Sitka,* make its trial run in San Francisco Bay. The vessel was built at Sitka, Alaska, by an American as a pleasure boat for officers of the Russian company. It was a side-wheel vessel, thirty-seven feet long, of nine-foot beam and drew eighteen inches of water.

PART IV

ARGONAUTS
(1848–1869)

PART IV

ARGONAUTS

(1848–1869)

VILLAINS and scoundrels . . . beardless youths and sophisticated adventurers. . . . French merchants and German travelers. . . . Australian convicts and South American gentlemen. . . . New England puritans and ladies of fancy. These were the Argonauts who heard in far places and near the stories of the Sierra's astounding golden wealth.

And so was initiated one of the most chaotic epochs that any land in the world has ever experienced. It was a time of strong men and deplorable excesses. By land and by sea these modern Jasons descended on California with the numbers and the fury of the Crusades.

They gutted the mountains of their golden wealth, denuded the forests, almost exterminated the wild things of the land and the air. Bacchus was rampant; a Saturnalia was abroad.

But the legion of Argonauts, despite the havoc they wrought, furnished a needed tonic constituent to the lethargic culture then existing. In the days of the gold rush, no coward ever started for California, and no weakling ever got there.

January 24, 1848—James Wilson Marshall discovered gold in the tail-race of a saw-mill he was building for John Sutter at Coloma, on the American River, thus precipitating the California gold rush of 1848-1850, which drew thousands of venturesome Argonauts from all parts of the world.

February 2, 1848—The Treaty of Guadalupe Hidalgo was signed at Guadalupe Hidalgo, Mexico, by representatives of the United States and Mexico, thus ending the Mexican War. New Mexico and California, Nevada, Utah, most of Arizona, and a part of Colorado were ceded by Mexico to the United States on payment of $15,000,000 by the United States and the assumption of $3,250,000, representing claims of American citizens against Mexico. The Río Grande and thence to the Pacific, south of San Diego, were accepted as the boundary lines between the two nations.

April 3, 1848—The first public school in California after the American occupation was opened on Portsmouth Square in San Francisco, under the direction of Thomas Douglas, a Yale graduate, and under the supervision of a committee consisting of William A. Leidesdorff, William S. Clark and William Glover. From this, has grown the public school system of California.

October 14, 1848—John Sutter transferred his property about Sutter's Fort to his son, John Sutter, Jr. Immediately thereafter, young Sutter founded the modern city of Sacramento along the embarcadero of the Sacramento River, three miles below the site of the original Sutterville. The city adopted its first charter October 13, 1849.

November 9, 1848—The first regular post office of the United States Post Office Department in California was established in San Francisco. Other offices were opened at Monterey, November 21, 1848, and at Los Angeles, April 9, 1850.

December 5, 1848—The publication of President James K. Polk's annual message authenticated the reported discovery of gold in California and gave impetus to the gold rush to California.

January 9, 1849—Naglee and Sinton, the former a West Point graduate who came to California with the New York Volunteers, and the latter a former paymaster on the U.S.S. *Ohio,* opened an "Exchange and Deposits Office" in the Parker House on Kearny Street in San Francisco, which proved to be California's first commercial bank.

February 26, 1849—Gen. Persifer F. Smith arrived in San Francisco to succeed Col. R. B. Mason as military commander of California and Oregon, and civil governor of California. He was superseded as civil gov-- ernor of California by Brig.-Gen. Bennett Riley, who arrived at Monterey April 12, 1849.

February 28, 1849—The *California,* first steamer placed in service by the Pacific Mail Steamship Company to carry mail and passengers on the route from New York to Chagres, thence across the Isthmus of Panamá, and from Panamá to San Francisco, arrived in San Francisco, bringing three hundred and sixty-five passengers and a crew of thirty-six. The *California* left Panamá on February 1. She was followed into San Francisco by the *Oregon,* and the *Panamá,* sister ships, which arrived on April 1, 1849, and June 4, 1849, respectively.

April 12, 1849—Brig.-Gen. Bennett Riley arrived at Monterey to assume the office of civil governor of California, under instructions of the Secretary of War of the United States. Riley succeeded Gen. Persifer F. Smith.

July 6, 1849—The first meeting of the commissioners appointed by the governments of the United States and Mexico to fix the boundary between the two republics from the Pacific Ocean eastward to El Paso, in accordance with the terms of the Treaty of Guadalupe Hidalgo, was held at San Diego. Commissioner for the United States was Col. John B. Weller; for Mexico, Pedro García Condé. Lieut.-Col. John C. Frémont was appointed to succeed Weller in June, 1849, but resigned almost immediately and Weller was renamed. John R. Bartlett superseded him in June, 1850, and the work of the commission was completed in September, 1851.

August 17, 1849—The first river steamboat in California, the *George Washington,* arrived at Sacramento from Benicia, inaugurating regular service between San Francisco Bay and the rapidly growing inland city.

August 29, 1849—The first accurate map of the city of Los Angeles, or "Plan de la Ciudad de los Angeles," was completed and filed after surveys made by Lieut. E. O. C. Ord, U.S.A., were terminated.

September 1, 1849—The convention called to write a constitution for California assembled in Colton Hall, Monterey. It consisted of forty-eight delegates and was presided over by Dr. Robert Semple. The constitution adopted was patterned mainly after those of New York and Iowa. Aside from the usual provisions for the protection of life and property, the election of State officials and the convening of a legislature, it fixed the boundary of the State and outlawed slavery. It was signed by all delegates October 13, 1849.

September 8, 1849—The First California Guard, premier organization of State troops in California, which later was to form the nucleus of the National Guard, was given official status when Brig.-Gen. Bennett Riley commissioned Henry M. Naglee as captain. Other officers sworn in were: William O. Howard and Myron Norton, first lieutenants; Hall McAllister and David F. Bagley, second lieutenants; Samuel Gerry, surgeon; and R. H. Sinton, sergeant. The guard first saw service in quelling the squatters' riots in Sacramento in 1850.

September 9, 1849—The first lodge of the I. O. O. F. in California, known as Lodge No. 1, was formally instituted at San Francisco, though members of the order had met informally as early as 1847.

October 10, 1849—Joint boundary commissions of the United States and Mexico established the southern border between Mexico and California, in N. Lat. 23-31-58-59 and W. Long. 7-48, 20-1 (a marine league south of the bay of San Diego), whence it was to run in a straight line easterly to the confluence of the Gila and Colorado rivers.

October 13, 1849—California's first constitution was adopted by delegates elected to a constitutional convention at Monterey. The constitution, similar to those of New York and Iowa, established the boundary of the State, provided for the election of executive, legislative and judicial officials, created a system of taxation and ordered the foundation of public schools.

October 18, 1849—The first theater in California, the Eagle Theater, a flimsy frame-and-canvas structure, opened at Sacramento, presenting *The Bandit Chief*.

October 25, 1849—The first meeting for the purpose of organizing the Democratic party in California was held in Portsmouth Square, San Francisco, with John W. Geary presiding. A lengthy statement of principles and resolutions was presented by William Van Voorhies. These advocated "the preservation of the Constitution inviolate . . . defeat of powerful and chartered monopolies, opposition to enactments intended to benefit the few at the expense of the many," and the approval of a policy that "would preserve the honor of the country when menaced, punish the offender when its rights were invaded and ever look forward to an honorable extension of the area of freedom." The party hurriedly nominated candidates for State office at a primary election on October 29, and succeeded in electing Peter H. Burnett as governor on November 13.

October 30, 1849—The first lodge of the Ancient Order of Free and Accepted Masons in California, Western Star No. 1, was founded at Benton City. The Grand Lodge was established in April, 1850.

November 13, 1849—By a vote of 12,064 to 811, voters of California ratified the State constitution adopted by the constitutional convention at Monterey on October 13. At the same time they elected Peter H. Burnett as first constitutional governor, and Edward Gilbert and George W. Wright, representatives in Congress.

December 17, 1849—The first California constitutional Legislature convened at San José. It consisted of sixteen senators and thirty-six assemblymen. E. Kirby Chamberlain was elected president pro tempore of the senate and Thomas J. White, speaker of the assembly. On December 20 the Legislature elected John C. Frémont and William M. Gwin, United States Senators. Before adjournment on April 22, 1850, it adopted a code of laws providing, among other things, for the creation of twenty-seven counties, the election of judges, the imposition of taxes, and the prohibition of slavery.

December 20, 1849—Humboldt Bay, frequently passed by mariners for three centuries but never described, was discovered from land by a party of eight miners led by Dr. Josiah Gregg, a frontiersman from New Mexico, who were seeking a better route for supplies from San Francisco to the mines on the Trinity River. Dissension prevailed during the course of the journey as the result of privations endured. After finding the bay, naming Eel and Mad rivers, and Van Duzen's fork, the party separated. Gregg died of starvation in the difficult journey back to the Sacramento Valley; the others survived. First to enter the bay by sea was Hans H. Buhne, second officer of the trading ship *Laura Virginia,* commanded by Lieut. Douglass Ottinger, who crossed the bar in a small boat April 9, 1850. Ottinger named it "Humboldt" for the German explorer, Alexander Humboldt.

December 20, 1849—Peter H. Burnett, who had emigrated from Missouri to Oregon in 1843, came to California in 1848 and worked for John Sutter, was inaugurated first American constitutional governor of California.

December 24, 1849—The first of six destructive fires

started in San Francisco in Denison's Exchange, burning the block bounded by Washington, Kearny, Clay and Montgomery streets, with the loss of fifty houses, valued at $1,250,000.

February 4, 1850—The Jayhawker party of overland emigrants, who had sought to reach California by a short-cut from Salt Lake which took them southward via Mountain Meadow and Death Valley, and who suffered great privations and hardships, losing thirteen members of the party in and about Death Valley, finally reached safety at the San Francisquito Ranch, near the present town of Newhall.

February 18, 1850—California's original counties, twenty-seven in number, were created by an act of the first California Legislature. They were: San Diego, Los Angeles, Santa Barbara, San Luís Obispo, Monterey, Branciforte (later known as Santa Cruz), San Francisco, Santa Clara, Contra Costa, Marin, Sonoma, Solano, Yola (later Yolo), Napa, Mendocino, Sacramento, El Dorado, Sutter, Yuba, Butte, Colusi (later

Colusa), Shasta, Trinity, Calaveras, San Joaquín, Tuolumne and Mariposa. These counties had in 1930 a population as follows: San Diego, 209,659; Los Angeles, 2,208,492; Santa Barbara, 65,167; San Luís Obispo, 29,613; Monterey, 53,705; Santa Cruz, 37,433; San Francisco, 634,394; Santa Clara, 145,118; Contra Costa, 78,608; Marin, 41,648; Sonoma, 62,222; Solano, 40,834; Yolo, 23,644; Napa, 22,897; Mendocino, 23,505; Sacramento, 141,999; El Dorado, 8,325; Sutter, 14,618; Yuba, 11,331; Butte, 34,093; Colusa, 10,258; Shasta, 13,927; Trinity, 2,809; Calaveras, 6,008; San Joaquín, 102,940; Tuolumne, 9,271; Mariposa, 3,233.

February 27, 1850—The city of Sacramento was incorporated. It took its name from the Río del Sacramento, explored in 1808 by Lieut. Gabriel Moraga. The present city, first known as Sutterville, was laid out by John A. Sutter, Jr., shortly after October 14, 1848, at the landing below his father's famous fort. In 1930 Sacramento had a population of 93,750, and an area of 14.27 square miles.

March 27, 1850—The city of San Diego was incorporated. First settlement on San Diego Bay occurred on May 17, 1769. A presidio was created in 1774, but civil government did not supplant military rule until 1835. The modern city has a population (1930) of 147,995, and an area of 94.65 square miles.

March 27, 1850—The city of San José was incorporated. San José is the first "city" to have been founded in California. It was established as a pueblo on November 29, 1777, by Gov. Felipe de Neve, and named in honor of Saint Joseph, patron saint of the sacred expedition of 1769, headed by Gaspar de Portolá and Father Junípero Serra. The modern city has a population of 57,651, and an area of 9.50 square miles.

March 27, 1850—Benicia, designed to be a rival to San Francisco as a port on San Francisco Bay, was incorporated.

April 1, 1850—San Francisco County government was instituted by the election of sheriff, county judge, recorder, surveyor, treasurer, assessor, coroner, county attorney, district attorney, county clerk, and clerk of the superior court. The county was geographically coincidental with the city, for which officials, including a mayor and a common council, were elected on May 1, 1850. San Francisco in 1930 had a population of 634,394.

April 4, 1850—The city of Los Angeles was incorporated. Founded early in September, 1781 (the date is not definitely known though it is generally believed to have been September 4), by orders of Gov. Felipe de Neve, the city was christened "El Pueblo de Nuestra Señora, la Reina de Los Angeles de Porciúncula (the city of Our Lady, Queen of the Angels of Porciúncula), for the site had been so named by Father Juan Crespí on August 2, 1769, in the course of the first land expedition in search of Monterey. In 1930 the city had a population of 1,238,048, and an area of 450.51 square miles.

April 15, 1850—The city of San Francisco was incorporated. The Bay of San Francisco was discovered by Sergt. José Ortega, attached to the first land expedition seeking Monterey, on November 2, 1769, though he failed to name it. The city takes its present name from the mission of San Francisco de Asís, founded by Fathers Francisco Palóu, Pedro Benito Cambón, José Nocedal, and Tomás de la Peña, October 9, 1776. The city had a population in 1930 of 634,394, and an area of 44.20 square miles.

April 22, 1850—The California Legislature adopted a law to protect the native Indians. Among other things, it confirmed them in the possession of their villages, permitted them to contract for their labor with the whites, but provided that in criminal cases, whites could not be convicted on their testimony.

April 23, 1850—John Glanton, operator of a crude ferry across the Colorado River at Yuma, widely utilized by gold-seeking emigrants bound for California via the southern emigrant trail, with twelve or fifteen other residents of the vicinity, were massacred by hostile Yuma Indians. The Indians, it later developed, were actuated to commit the wholesale murders because Glanton and his companions had stolen their ferry-boat, imposed upon them in many ways, and treated them cruelly.

May 4, 1850—Second of six destructive fires started in San Francisco, in the United States Exchange, a gambling resort, burning three blocks between Montgomery, Dupont, Jackson and Clay streets, consuming 300 buildings with a loss of $4,000,000.

June 14, 1850—The third of six destructive fires started in San Francisco in the Sacramento House, burning the area between Clay and California streets, from Kearny Street to the waterfront, with a loss of $3,000,000.

August 14, 1850—Climaxing a lengthy contest between Americans, mainly from the Missouri border, who had illegally seized numerous parcels of land in and about Sacramento under the pretext that title to them originating in a Mexican grant to Sutter was invalid, and who had defied proper court orders for ejectments, armed squatters clashed with public officials in Sacramento, in what has since come to be known as the "Sacramento squatters' riot," with a loss of four killed and five wounded. The death of the squatters' leaders temporarily ended the conflict, but the affair is regarded as marking the inception of squatterism and a general challenging of Mexican land titles in California.

August 31, 1850—The Society of California Pioneers, with membership restricted to residents of, and arrivals in, California prior to January 1, 1849, was organized in San Francisco. A second class of members, comprising United States citizens arriving between January 1, 1849, and January 1, 1850, later were admitted to the society, which was reorganized July 6, 1853.

September 9, 1850—President Millard Fillmore signed a bill adopted by the United States Senate on August 13 by a vote of 34 to 18, and by the House of Representatives on September 7, by a vote of 150 to 56, admitting California to the Union as a State.

September 17, 1850—The fourth of six destructive fires started in San Francisco in the Philadelphia

House, burning the area bounded by Dupont, Montgomery, Washington and Pacific streets, with a loss of $500,000.

September 20, 1850—Congress appropriated $90,000 for the construction of California's first six lighthouses at Alcatraz Island, the entrance of San Francisco Bay, on the Farallones, at Monterey, Point Concepción, and San Diego. The sites were located by engineers conducting a survey for the Coast Survey Department, headed by George Davidson.

October 18, 1850—First news of admission of California to the Union reached San Francisco with the arrival of the mail steamer *Oregon*. Overjoyed, the people engaged in a frenzied impromptu celebration, business being suspended, a procession formed, and bands played. A formal celebration of the event occurred on October 29 when a new star was added to the flag flying in the plaza.

November 27, 1850—Camp Independence at the junction of the Gila and Colorado rivers was established to protect California emigrants from attack by hostile Yuma Indians. In March, 1851, the camp became known as Fort Yuma. Major S. P. Heintzelman commanded the outpost.

January 9, 1851—Peter H. Burnett resigned as first American constitutional governor of California and was succeeded by Lieut.-Gov. John McDougal, "a gentlemanly drunkard, and democratic politician of the order for which California was destined to become somewhat unpleasantly notorious." Burnett was born at Nashville, Tennessee, November 15, 1807, emigrated to Missouri in 1817, and to Oregon in 1843, where he aided in improving the provisional government, becoming a judge of the Supreme Court, serving from 1845 to 1848 when he led an overland party to California. Here he became attorney for Sutter. He was the Democratic party's first candidate for governor and California's first constitutional governor. He retired from public life and continued the practice of law. He died at San Francisco May 17, 1895.

January 31, 1851—The first orphan asylum in California, the San Francisco Orphan Asylum, was founded by Protestants.

February 5, 1851—Marysville, founded by Theodore Cordua and known as New Mecklenburg and Yubaville, was incorporated as a city.

March 3, 1851—The Congress of the United States passed a bill establishing a Land Commission to investigate the validity of all Spanish and Mexican land grants in California, and to confirm titles thereto. Until March 1, 1856, when the commission disbanded, it examined 813 claims. Of these 591 were finally confirmed, and 203 rejected. Of the 813 claims, 264 were settled by the commission, 450 were adjudicated by the district courts, and 99 by the United States Supreme Court.

March 19, 1851—As a result of negotiations between a Federal government commission composed of Redick McKee, G. W. Barbour and O. M. Wozencraft, the first of a series of peace treaties with hostile California Indians was signed. The first treaty involved six tribes on the Tuolumne, Merced and Mariposa rivers, followed by ten similar ones with 123 tribes in other sections of the State. After impartial investigation, the commission declared that by far the greatest share of the Indian troubles could be traced to white aggression, or broken promises. Treaties provided for the establishment of the Indians on reservations and their care and support by the government for one year. Many abuses crept into their supervision.

March 25, 1851—Maj. James D. Savage, in command of the volunteer Mariposa Battalion, pursuing hostile Indians who had raided trading posts in the San Joaquín Valley, discovered Yosemite Valley. The battalion first saw the valley from the present Inspiration Point, later camping at the base of El Capitán. Dr. L. H. Bunnell, surgeon for the battalion, proposed the name "Yosemite" after the tribal name of the Indians living there.

April 22, 1851—California's long-famous and still-operative Homestead Law was signed by Gov. John McDougal. The law provided briefly that any home and a reasonable amount of land pertaining thereto, continuously occupied by a citizen as his dwelling place, was exempt from forced sale on account of debts.

April 25, 1851—Nevada County was created by legislative enactment from the southern and eastern part of Yuba County. Nevada County in 1930 had a population of 10,596.

April 25, 1851—Klamath County was created by legislative enactment. Originally it was composed of that part of the State lying north of a line drawn east from the mouth of Mad River and west of the summit of the Coast Range. It was dissolved under an act of the Legislature of March 28, 1874 and bears the distinction of being the only county in the State which has completely disappeared.

April 25, 1851—Placer County was created by legislative enactment from portions of Yuba and Sutter counties. Placer County in 1930 had a population of 24,468.

May 3, 1851—The fifth, and worst, of six destructive fires started in San Francisco in the upholstery and paint establishment of Baker and Messerve, burning all the business district between Pine and Pacific streets, from Kearny Street to the Battery, a total of more than 22 blocks, with a loss of from 1,000 to 2,000 structures, valued at $12,000,000.

May 17, 1851—The first issue of Los Angeles' first newspaper, *La Estrella de los Angeles,* or *The Los Angeles Star,* was published. The first issue was composed of four pages, 12 x 18 inches in size, two pages being printed in English and two in Spanish. The English editor was John A. Lewis and the Spanish editor was Manuel Clemente Rojo. In 1933, Henry R. Wagner, geographer and historian, reproduced a facsimile of the first issue of the *Star* for distribution among his friends.

May 26, 1851—Fort Miller, named for Major Albert S. Miller, was established on the San Joaquín River and occupied by two companies of the Second United States Infantry to protect miners from the hostile tribes of San Joaquín Indians. The post was abandoned October 1, 1864.

June 9, 1851—The first Vigilance Committee of San Francisco was formed, with Sam Brannan as president of the executive committee. First victim of the vigilantes was John Jenkins, arraigned the day following on charges of stealing a safe, and who was promptly found guilty and hanged from the veranda of the old City Hotel. The first committee before its retirement in September hanged four malefactors and exiled more than fifty.

June 22, 1851—The sixth of six destructive fires started in San Francisco in a dwelling on the north side of Pacific Street, below Powell, burning over an area bounded by Clay, Broadway, Sansome and Powell streets, covering all or part of 16 blocks, with a loss of 450 structures, valued at $2,500,000.

August 31, 1851—The *Flying Cloud,* built by Donald McKay and commanded by Capt. Josiah Perkins Creesy, arrived at San Francisco, having made the voyage from New York via Cape Horn in 81 days, 21 hours, an all-time record for sailing ships. The *Flying Cloud* is said to have bettered this record at a later date but this achievement has never been satisfactorily verified.

January 8, 1852—John Bigler, third American constitutional governor of California, was inaugurated. He succeeded John McDougal, who was born in Ohio in 1818, served in the Mexican War, and arrived in California in 1849. He was a delegate to the constitutional convention and was elected lieutenant-governor in 1849. His administration was ludicrous, historians agreeing that he was wholly unfitted for the office, and could never have succeeded to it save for Burnett's resignation which placed him there automatically. On his retirement from the governorship he never again held an important public office. He died in San Francisco March 30, 1866.

March 22, 1852—Siskiyou County was created by legislative enactment from the northern portion of Shasta County and a part of Klamath County. Siskiyou County in 1930 had a population of 25,480.

April 16, 1852—Sierra County was created by legislative enactment from the eastern portion of Yuba

County. Sierra County in 1930 had a population of 2,422.

April 20, 1852—The California State Legislature divided Mariposa County, creating Tulare County from its southern portion. Tulare County in 1930 had a population of 77,442.

April 21, 1852—The city of Stockton was incorporated. Stockton was founded in 1847 by Charles M. Weber, under the name of Tuleburg. Later it was known as New Albany and finally it was given the name of Stockton to honor Com. Robert F. Stockton. The city in 1930 had a population of 47,963, and an area of 9.94 square miles.

May 4, 1852—The city of Oakland was incorporated. It was founded in 1850 by squatters headed by A. J. Moon, Horace W. Carpentier and E. Adams, who settled on Rancho San Antonio granted in 1820 to Luís Peralta. Oakland had a population in 1930 of 284,063, and an area of 53.16 square miles.

November 11, 1852—E. F. Beale was appointed by President Millard Fillmore as General Superintendent of Indian Affairs for California. The treaties of 1851 had failed to pacify the aborigines and there followed the Klamath War of 1851-1852, conflict with the Indians of Honey Lake Valley and the Coast Range tribes in 1858-1859, and the Pitt River campaign of 1867. Not until the Modoc War of 1873 was terminated was a permanent peace effected between the California Indians and the whites. Beale's task was a Herculean one, faced as he was with the opposition of Indians and whites alike, and he was replaced by Col. T. J. Henley long before the Indian troubles were over.

January 19, 1853—Stephen Mallory White was born in San Francisco. He became a Los Angeles attorney, district attorney of Los Angeles County, State senator, lieutenant-governor of California and United States Senator. He is remembered chiefly for his fight for the San Pedro site for Los Angeles' harbor against Collis P. Huntington who favored Santa Monica. He died February 21, 1901, in Los Angeles.

March 3, 1853—Agitation for a Pacific railroad, which had started as early as 1835 and continued incessantly, led Congress to authorize the Secretary of War to employ army topographical engineers to ascertain the most economical and practicable route for a railroad from the Mississippi River to the Pacific Ocean, and appropriated $150,000 to defray expenses. The survey was started in the spring of 1853. The work required several years and five routes were examined, notably from St. Paul to Vancouver, Washington; Council Bluffs to Benicia, California; Westport, Indiana, to San Francisco; Fort Smith, Arkansas to San Pedro, and Fulton, Missouri to San Pedro. The reports presented all the facts but omitted definite conclusions as to the superiority of one route over the others.

March 12, 1853—Humboldt County was created by legislative enactment from territory which previously had been part of Trinity County. Humboldt County in 1930 had a population of 43,233.

March 25, 1853—Alameda County was formed from portions of Contra Costa and Santa Clara counties. Alameda County in 1930 had a population of 474,883.

March 30, 1853—A California law was enacted imposing a tax of $4.00 a month on "foreign miners." The measure was aimed especially at the Chinese.

April 26, 1853—San Bernardino County was created by legislative enactment from the eastern portion of Los Angeles County. San Bernardino County in 1930 had a population of 133,900.

July 25, 1853—Joaquín Murieta, notorious California bandit who had turned brigand as a result of his persecution by American miners, was shot and killed by Capt. Harry S. Love, leader of a company of rangers organized for the purpose of apprehending him. Murieta had operated as a brigand but two years when he was killed, but during that period had robbed and murdered from one end of California to the other. He was shot on the plains of San Joaquín Valley, west of Tulare Lake.

September 22, 1853—The first telegraph in California, connecting the lighthouse at Point Lobos with San Francisco, a distance of eight miles, was opened.

November 3, 1853—William Walker, "gray-eyed man of destiny," with 48 filibuster followers, recruited in San Francisco, whence he had sailed on October 16, 1853, captured La Paz, Lower California and proclaimed the Republic of Lower California. He was soon repulsed and driven from the peninsula. Later in 1855-1860, he led other filibuster campaigns in Nicaragua and Honduras. These ultimately failed and Walker was executed in Honduras in 1860.

January 9, 1854—Major-Gen. John E. Wool was given command of the Department of the Pacific of the United States Army, which had only shortly before been created, and which embraced all of the United

States west of the Rocky Mountains, excepting Utah and New Mexico.

February 25, 1854—The fifth session of the California State Legislature permanently located the State capital at Sacramento. In the interim between the meeting of the first Legislature in San José in 1849, legislative sessions had been held in Vallejo and Benicia.

March 18, 1854—Plumas County was created by legislative enactment from the eastern portion of Butte County. Plumas County in 1930 had a population of 7,913.

April 3, 1854—A branch of the United States Mint was opened in San Francisco, designed mainly to coin gold. Its establishment ended private coinage which had resulted in the circulation of gold coins of varying weights and quality.

April 5, 1854—Stanislaus County was created by legislative enactment from territory which had previously been included in Tuolumne County. Stanislaus County in 1930 had a population of 56,641.

April 13, 1854—The city of San Bernardino was incorporated. San Bernardino was founded by a colony of 500 Mormons from Salt Lake City under the leadership of Elders Amasa M. Lyman and Charles C. Rich in 1851 on a section of Rancho San Bernardino known as "Agua Caliente." The Mormons re-named the community "San Bernardino" from the old *asistencia* of Misión San Gabriel which was located nearby. The city in 1930 had a population of 37,481 and an area of 18.07 square miles.

May 10, 1854—Amador County was formed by legislative enactment from that portion of Calaveras County north of the Mokelumne River. Amador County in 1930 had a population of 8,494.

May 13, 1854—Placerville, discovered in 1848, originally known as "Old Dry Diggins," and later as "Hangtown" and "Ravine City," was incorporated.

May 13, 1854—The State Agricultural Society was formed in Sacramento to conduct fairs, exhibitions, etc., and to otherwise promote agriculture, horticulture and stock-raising in California. F. W. Macondray was its first president.

August 10, 1854—Fort Tejon, near the summit of the Tejon Pass, was established to protect settlers and transient whites in the southern San Joaquín Valley from hostile Indians. Among the military forces that occupied it was Company A, of the United States Dragoons. The fort was abandoned September 11, 1864.

October 6, 1854—Henry Meiggs, developer of the North Beach area in San Francisco, alderman of the city, and first of California's high-pressure subdividers and realtors, fled to the South Seas, and ultimately to South America, to avoid arrest on charges of forging city warrants. In Peru and Chile he made a fortune in railroad building, made due restitution for his fraudulent transactions which totalled thousands, and in 1873-1874 the California Legislature, over the veto of Gov. Newton Booth, granted him amnesty. Meiggs feared Booth's wrath, doubted the legality of the action of the Legislature, and remained in South America, dying in Lima in 1877.

February 22, 1855—A run upon the bank of Page,

Bacon and Company, forced it to close, thus initiating California's first major panic. Subsequently a number of financial institutions, including Adams and Company, were forced to suspend. Before recovery occurred, two years later, business failures totalled hundreds, losses ran into many millions and California's credit reputation suffered all over the world.

April 19, 1855—Merced County was created by legislative enactment from the western portion of Mariposa County. Merced County in 1930 had a population of 36,748.

August 7, 1855—The "Know Nothing," or "American," party, a secret political organization with a platform based chiefly on opposition to foreigners and foreign immigration, held its first State convention in California at Sacramento. The organization had been exceedingly active since early in 1854, had chapters in many villages and mining-camps, and had carried municipal elections in Marysville, Sacramento and elsewhere. The party nominated J. Neely Johnson for governor; Robert M. Johnson for lieutenant-governor, and Hugh C. Murray and David S. Terry for justices of the State Supreme Court. All candidates were swept into office at the election on September 5. The party took its name from the fact that when members were asked about it by non-members they were pledged to "know nothing" about it. The party was especially anti-Catholic, and anti-Chinese, and sponsored much legislation restricting the liberties of the celestials.

January 9, 1856—John Neely Johnson, first gubernatorial candidate of the native "American," or "Know Nothing," party was inaugurated California's fourth

American constitutional governor. He succeeded John Bigler, who was born in Pennsylvania January 8, 1805, became a printer, editor and lawyer, and emigrated to California in 1849. He entered the State assembly in 1850, becoming its speaker, later joining forces with David C. Broderick which resulted in his election as governor. He was re-elected, September 7, 1853. His administration was marked by anti-negro and anti-Chinese legislation, State printing office and State hospital extravagance scandals, and the rise of the "Know Nothing" party. Bigler was United States Minister to Chile, 1847-1861, returned to California, where he held several minor political offices, and died at Sacramento November 29, 1871.

February 22, 1856—The first railroad in California, the Sacramento Valley Railroad Company, operating between Sacramento and Folsom, was formally opened.

April 9, 1856—Tehama County was created by legislative enactment from portions of Colusa, Butte and Shasta counties. Tehama County in 1930 had a population of 13,866.

April 19, 1856—Fresno County was created by legislative enactment from territory which previously composed the southern part of Merced and the southern and eastern part of Mariposa counties. Fresno County had a population of 144,379 in 1930.

April 19, 1856—San Mateo County was created by legislative enactment from the southern part of San Francisco County. San Mateo County in 1930 had a population of 77,405.

April 19, 1856—San Francisco city and county were consolidated, and a government established designed to abolish corruption, increase order and efficiently minister to the public welfare.

April 26, 1856—Settlers in Honey Lake Valley in northeastern California at a mass meeting arbitrarily declared the region to have seceded from the State of California—and to be known henceforth as the "Territory of Nataqua." Leaders in the movement, which quickly proved abortive and a failure, were Peter Lassen and Isaac Roop.

May 14, 1856—The assassination of James King of William, editor of the *Evening Bulletin,* a crusader against crime and corrupt politics, by James Casey, ex-convict and politician, on this date, led to the formation the following day of the San Francisco Vigilance Committee of 1856, with William T. Coleman as president. Composed of 8,000 members, the committee hung Casey, defied corrupt public officials, including the governor, executed four offenders, and deported twenty-five others before it disbanded on August 21.

August 23, 1856—The first wagon-road over the

Sierra Nevada, between Murphy's, California, and Carson Valley, Nevada, was opened to traffic. The road was financed by public and private contributions, and proceeded through the north fork of the Stanislaus River, Indian Valley, Twin Lakes, Fitch Valley, and Carson Canyon.

March 2, 1857—Del Norte County was formed by legislative enactment from a portion of Klamath County. Del Norte County in 1930 had a population of 4,739.

August 31, 1857—First stage of the San Antonio and San Diego stage line, popularly known as "The Jackass Mail," premier overland stage route and forerunner of the Butterfield Overland Mail, arrived in San Diego. The mail line was operated first on a twice-a-month schedule, then on a weekly, until August 2, 1861, when it was discontinued. When at the height of its operations, the average trip from San Diego to San Antonio, or vice versa, consumed 21 days.

January 8, 1858—A corps of 14 camels, which it was hoped would prove practical for transportation of mails to California across the deserts of the Southwest, arrived in Los Angeles on its first journey from Albuquerque, New Mexico, in charge of Lieut. E. F. Beale. Though the corps made several subsequent journeys, the camels proved so intractable that the corps was disbanded in 1860 and finally set free in Arizona.

January 8, 1858—John B. Weller was inaugurated fifth American constitutional governor of California. He succeeded J. Neely Johnson, who was born in Indiana, August 2, 1825, studied law, came to California in

1849, participated in the Mariposa Indian War, was elected to the Legislature of 1853 and governor in 1856. His administration saw the passage of additional anti-Chinese legislation, the imposition of miners' taxes, attempts to establish the Territory of Nataqua, and the struggle between Broderick and Terry, with its fatal duel. Retiring as governor, Johnson resumed the practice of law, moved to Nevada with the Comstock rush and there again entered politics, finally becoming justice of the Supreme Court of Nevada in 1867. He died of sunstroke at Salt Lake City on August 31, 1872.

September 15, 1858—The first coaches of the Butterfield Overland Mail left simultaneously from the eastern termini (Tipton, Missouri and Little Rock,

Arkansas) and the western terminus (San Francisco). The stage line operated under a government mail subsidy of $600,000 a year, on a weekly schedule and averaged 23 days for each one-way journey. The southern route was abandoned by order of Congress, March 2, 1861, and John Butterfield, founder of the line, was given a new contract to carry the mails between the

Mississippi River and California via the Central Route on a 17-day schedule.

April 18, 1859—The California Legislature authorized the people of the six counties of San Luís Obispo, Santa Barbara, Los Angeles, San Diego, San Bernardino and a part of Buena Vista—all the State south of the 36th parallel—to vote upon State division, as a result of complaints from the southerners of burdensome taxation and unfair representation. The Legislature of 1860 opposed the move and the desired State division never eventuated.

September 13, 1859—David C. Broderick, United States Senator from California, elected on an anti-slavery platform six days before, was mortally shot in a duel by David S. Terry, who had resigned from the California Supreme Court to challenge the Senator. Terry charged that Broderick had grossly insulted him in a political convention three months previously during Terry's advocacy of the campaign of Broderick's opponent, William M. Gwin. The duel occurred near Black Point, in San Mateo County.

December 12, 1859—Senator William M. Gwin in a debate on slavery and secession in the Senate inferred that if the Southern States seceded, California would establish a Pacific Republic. This created much discussion, various professions of loyalty to the Union and to the South by the adherents of both and, finally, the raising of a Pacific Republic flag on board a surveying schooner at Stockton, January 16, 1861. But on May 17, 1861, the California Legislature pledged the State to the Union, and though the project of a Pacific Republic remained alive for a time, ultimately it was abandoned.

January 10, 1860—Milton S. Latham was inaugurated California's sixth governor after the American occupation. Latham held office but a few days, for the day after his inauguration the Legislature chose him as United States Senator to fill the office left vacant by the death of David C. Broderick. Latham succeeded John B. Weller, who was born February 12, 1812, at Montgomery, Ohio, studied law, and was elected to Congress for three successive terms from Butler County, Ohio. As a member of the Mexican Boundary Commission, he came to California in 1849, was elected United States Senator to succeed Frémont in 1852, and governor in 1858. On leaving the governorship, which saw much slavery and anti-slavery agitation, he was appointed United States Minister to Chile, a post he held from 1860 to 1861. He died in New Orleans, August 7, 1875.

January 14, 1860—John G. Downey was inaugurated as California's seventh American constitutional governor. Downey, a native of Ireland, came to California in 1849, and in 1850 opened a drug store in Los Angeles —the only establishment of the sort between San Francisco and San Diego. Later he engaged in stock-raising. His administration as governor was universally commended. It witnessed the establishment of the Pony Express and the Overland Stage, and California's adherence to the Union during the Civil War. Retiring as governor, Downey returned to Los Angeles, engaged in banking, and did much for the development of the

Southland. He ran for governor again in 1863, but was defeated by Frederick F. Low. He died in Los Angeles, March 1, 1894.

April 14, 1860—The first rider of the famous Pony Express reached San Francisco from St. Joseph, Missouri. The Pony Express, organized by W. H. Russell, was designed to speed valuable mails between the Mississippi River and California. The average time in transit was ten and one-half days. The express operated by relays. Each horse was ridden about 24 miles; each rider rode 72 miles. The charge for carrying letters was $5 per half-ounce. The service was abandoned in November, 1861, with the advent of the overland telegraph. The express boasted such noted horsemen as "Pony Bob" Haslam and William F. "Buffalo Bill" Cody.

October 8, 1860—The first telegraph line between San Francisco and Los Angeles was opened with a flowery congratulatory message from H. D. Barrows to the *San Francisco Bulletin*.

February 15, 1861—Fort Point, on the site of the present San Francisco presidio, was occupied for the first time by American troops. At the outbreak of the Civil War the only fortifications on the coast of California and Oregon were at Fort Point and at Alcatraz Island.

April 1, 1861—The California Legislature adopted an act providing for the development of the grape and wine industry which resulted in California becoming the leading wine-producing State in the Union. Chairman of the viticulture commission authorized was A.

Haraszthy who, on a journey through Europe, collected and shipped back to California 100,000 vines of 1,400 varieties, with which the principal vineyards of the State were established.

April 19, 1861—Gen. Albert Sidney Johnston resigned as commander of the United States Army's Department of the Pacific. Johnston, a Confederate sympathizer, is generally believed to have accepted the command to enable him to deliver the fortifications and military forces of the Pacific to the rebel cause on the declaration of war between the States. Learning that his plans were known, he resigned before he could be removed. Johnston was killed at the Battle of Shiloh, April 6-7, 1862.

April 21, 1861—On the call of President Lincoln for volunteers to the Union Army, the California Regiment was formed at a meeting at the Metropolitan Hotel in New York City. E. D. Baker was chosen colonel; Brainard, lieutenant-colonel; Lemon, major; and Ross A. Fish, captain.

April 24, 1861—On a call of the Secretary of War, Gov. Downey ordered one regiment of infantry (the First California Infantry Volunteers), and five companies of cavalry (the First California Cavalry Volunteers), enlisted and placed at the service of Gen. Sumner in the Union Army. Subsequently there were enlisted: on August 14, 1861, four regiments of infantry and one of cavalry; in 1863, seven companies of cavalry and six companies, constituting the First Battalion of California Mountaineers; in 1863-1864, the First Battalion of Native California Cavalry; in 1863-

1864-1865, three other regiments, known as the Sixth, Seventh and Eighth California Infantry Volunteers. California volunteers never saw service east of the Rockies.

April 24, 1861—Mono County was created by legislative enactment from portions of Calaveras and Fresno counties. Mono County in 1930 had a population of 1,360.

May 17, 1861—The California Legislature pledged the State to the Union, following the receipt of news on April 24 that Fort Sumter had surrendered. The legislative resolution, almost unanimously adopted, declared that the people of the State were devoted to the Constitution and the Union, and were ready at all times to maintain the rights and the honor of the national government at home and abroad.

May 20, 1861—Lake County was created by legislative enactment from the portion of Napa County lying around Clear Lake. In 1930 Lake County had a population of 7,166.

June 28, 1861—The Central Pacific Railroad Company of California, destined to build the first transcontinental railroad, was organized, with Leland Stanford as president; Collis P. Huntington, vice-president; Mark Hopkins, treasurer; James Benley, secretary; T. D. Judah, chief engineer; and, with those above named, E. B. Crocker, John F. Morse, D. W. Strong, and Charles Marsh, directors. The capital stock of the company was $8,500,000.

October 24, 1861—The overland telegraph line built westward from Omaha and eastward from Placerville, was joined at Salt Lake City and the first transcontinental message was transmitted. The line was built by the Western Union Company under an annual subsidy for ten years of $40,000 a year, plus a grant of a quarter-section of land for every fifteen miles of line constructed.

November 14, 1861—Ex-Senator William M. Gwin and Atty.-Gen. Calhoun Benham, sympathizers with the Rebel cause and the secession movement, were arrested by Gen. Edwin A. Sumner on the *Orizaba* en route from California to Panamá. They were charged with treason, but after a short imprisonment were released for lack of evidence. Gwin and Benham destroyed incriminating maps and papers after their arrest.

January 10, 1862—Leland Stanford was inaugurated as California's eighth American constitutional governor. He was born March 19, 1824, in Albany, New York, and came to California in 1852. Stanford was first president of the Central Pacific Railroad Company, later settled at Palo Alto and eventually endowed the Leland Stanford Jr. University to honor his son. Stanford was California's "war governor," administering the State during the first two years of the Civil War. Though not a spectacular figure, he is generally regarded as an exceedingly competent executive.

July 1, 1862—President Abraham Lincoln signed a bill providing for the construction of the Union Pacific Railroad from the Missouri River to the Pacific Ocean under a government subsidy consisting of a free right-of-way, necessary timber, stone and earth from the public domain, and five alternate sections of public land per mile along the route of the road. Moreover, the government agreed to issue United States bonds to the builders in the sum of $16,000 for each mile of road built, payable in thirty years. The limit of cost of the project was placed at $50,000,000. On July 2, 1864, onerous provisions of the law were modified by Congress.

September 8, 1862—The San Francisco Stock and Exchange Board, first of several similar trading marts, was founded in San Francisco. The membership fee in the beginning was $100 and the board started business with 33 members. It was followed by the California Stock and Exchange Board in 1872, and the Pacific Stock Exchange in 1875. Here were bought and sold in frenzy and chaos the stocks of the famous Virginia City mines which made rich men out of many, and paupers of many more.

February 22, 1863—Having accepted, on December 1, 1862, the stipulations set up by act of Congress for the construction of the Union Pacific Railroad, the Central Pacific Railroad Company started work on the project. The first shovel of earth was turned at Sacramento by Gov. Leland Stanford, who was likewise president of the Central Pacific, in the presence of the State Legislature and other spectators.

March 15, 1863—The schooner *J. M. Chapman* was seized in San Francisco Bay and five men—Ridgeley Greathouse, Asbury Harpending, Alfred Rubery, William C. Law and Lorenzo C. Libby—were arrested as privateers. The first three were convicted when it was shown in court that they planned to prey upon Panamá mail steamers under a letter of marque from Jefferson Davis, president of the Confederacy, authorizing them to "burn, bond or take" any vessel of the United States or its citizens. Later President Lincoln pardoned them, and the vessel and its cargo was sold, the proceeds being distributed between the United States and the *Chapman's* captors.

April 20, 1863—Discovery of a small quantity of gold on Santa Catalina Island inaugurated a miniature gold rush and the formation of the San Pedro Mining District, with the promulgation of a code of mining laws "for the government of the locators of veins or lodes of quartz, or other rock containing precious metals, and ores, gold, silver, copper, galena or other minerals or mines that may be discovered, taken up, or located in Los Angeles County, San Pedro District, State of California." No gold in commercial quantities was found and the last claim was filed in 1865.

December 10, 1863—Frederick F. Low was inaugurated as California's ninth American constitutional governor. Low was born at Frankfort, Maine, on January 30, 1828, came to California in 1849, engaged in mining, was one of the founders of the California Steam Navigation Company, and established a banking business at Marysville. Low died in San Francisco July 21, 1894.

March 4, 1864—The Rev. Thomas Starr King, who is credited with saving California to the Union during the Civil War, died in San Francisco. King was born in New York in 1824, and was ordained as a Universalist preacher in Charleston, Mass., in 1846. In 1860 he came to San Francisco as pastor of the First Unitarian Church. Being an ardent Unionist, he immediately plunged into the then-raging fight over secession which threatened to put California into the Confederacy. His impassioned oratory and eloquent appeals for loyalty are believed to have prevented this. Later he was the prime mover in the organization here of the Sanitary Commission, the "Red Cross" of the Civil War.

March 16, 1864—Alpine County was created by legislative enactment from territory which had previously been portions of El Dorado, Amador, Calaveras and Tuolumne counties. The county's boundaries never have changed. Alpine County in 1930 had a population of 241. It is the smallest county, in population, in the United States.

April 1, 1864—Lassen County was created by legislative enactment from territory previously included in Plumas and Shasta counties. Lassen County in 1930 had a population of 12,589.

December 20, 1865—California ratified the Thirteenth Amendment to the Constitution of the United States, abolishing slavery.

March 22, 1866—Inyo County was created by legislative enactment. In 1930 it had a population of 6,555.

April 2, 1866—Kern County was created by legislative enactment from portions of Tulare and Los Angeles counties. Kern County in 1930 had a population of 82,570.

May 13, 1867—Workingmen of San Francisco in convention initiated a movement for a universal eight-hour day in California. The California Legislature in 1868 gave the movement impetus by making the eight-hour day for skilled labor legal. The shortened labor period was designed to secure leisure for the mental and physical improvement of the people, and to spread employment.

December 5, 1867—Henry H. Haight was inaugurated tenth American constitutional governor of California. Haight was born in Rochester, New York, was graduated from Yale, studied law, and in 1847 was admitted to the bar. He came to California in 1850. In politics he was particularly antipathetic to railroad subsidies. Haight died at San Francisco, September 2, 1878.

March 23, 1868—The University of California was established by act of the California Legislature. The university absorbed as its nucleus the College of California, founded by Henry Durant in Oakland in 1855. The university was financed from a congressional land-grant, the sale of San Francisco Bay tide-lands, specific appropriations by the Legislature, and gifts from individuals. At the outset it was provided that equal educational facilities should be furnished for both sexes and that military training should be compulsory for male students.

PART V

IRON HORSES
(1869–1885)

IRON HORSES

(1869–1885)

GOLD poured forth from California in a ceaseless stream. Into the vaults of financiers and bankers in Boston, New York, Washington, and Philadelphia it passed, to alter appreciably the whole economic structure of the still young Union and to color the lives and stimulate the imagination of an entire nation. "California" had become a magical word—the proverbial pot at the end of the rainbow was indeed a distinct reality in the remote and distant land where the sun set into the Pacific.

The clumps of primitive and disheveled dwellings that long huddled in disarrayed communities in the laps of Sierran gulches gradually took on a new form, and attained the dignity and the order of cities. The one-time remote province of New Spain overnight hung its star in the Union and took its place beside far older and much more substantial Commonwealths.

But the new State suffered in isolation, far removed from the centers of government, of commerce, of industry, and of finance. Formidable mountains, endless prairies and wide deserts, gave it a detachment that neither it nor its fellows in the Union of States wanted. Communication and transportation became the need, yea the prime essential to its welfare. There followed, as a consequence, the heroic though tragically pitiable Pony Express, and the equally unsatisfactory Overland Stage. The problem was a challenge to American inventiveness and the challenge was met. The first epochal event was the completion of the overland telegraph, and the second, the driving of the golden spike with the silver hammer at Promontory Point, Utah, which marked the beginning of the first transcontinental railway and the ending forever of California's isolation.

Iron horses dancing magically on copper wires; iron horses clattering rhythmically on steel rails had performed the miracle. The hoof-beats of "Pony Bob" Haslam and "Buffalo Bill" Cody had vanished into the somber shadows of forgotten canyons.

May 10, 1869—The Union Pacific Railroad, building west from Omaha, and the Central Pacific Railroad, building east from Sacramento, met at Promontory

Point, Utah, thus completing the first transcontinental railroad in the United States. The event was celebrated by appropriate ceremonies, including the placing at the junction of a tie of California laurel carrying a silver plate containing the names of officials and directors of both companies, and the driving of a golden spike by President Leland Stanford of the Central Pacific. On May 11, cars brought from the east over the Union Pacific were attached to President Stanford's special train and headed westward—the first train to make a transcontinental journey.

April 4, 1870—An act of the Legislature provided for the complete codification of California laws. The work was finally accomplished by a commission composed of Creed Hammond, John C. Burch and Charles A. Tuttle. Thus California secured the first complete code ever adopted by any English-speaking people.

October 24, 1871—The notorious "Chinese Massacre" occurred in Los Angeles, when a mob of five hundred angry Angelinos, failing to locate a much-sought Chinese criminal in Nigger Alley, seized and lynched eighteen innocent celestials and looted Chinatown.

December 8, 1871—Newton Booth was inaugurated as the eleventh American constitutional governor of California. Booth was born in Salem, Indiana, December 30, 1825, was educated at Asbury University, studied law at Terre Haute, came to California first in 1850, returned to Terre Haute in 1857, and finally settled permanently at Sacramento in 1860. Highly regarded professionally, he amassed a fortune in mercantile transactions. Booth resigned as governor February 27, 1875, to serve for six years as United States Senator from California. He died at Sacramento July 14, 1892.

March 7, 1872—The city of Alameda was incorporated. Originally known as "Bolsa de Encinal," or "Encinal de San Antonio," Alameda originally was a part of Rancho San Antonio granted in 1820 to Luís Peralta. A large tract of land was sold in 1850 by A. M. Peralta, one of the heirs, to W. W. Chipman and G. Auginbaugh, who, in turn disposed of half of it to another group, including H. S. Fitch, who laid out and sold the first town lots. In 1930 Alameda had a population of 35,033, and an area of 7.43 square miles.

March 27, 1872—Ventura County was created by legislative enactment from the eastern portion of Santa Barbara County. Ventura County in 1930 had a population of 54,976.

March 26, 1872—One of California's most destructive earthquakes centered in the Owens Valley, killing or injuring sixty persons at Lone Pine, wrecking the town, as well as the towns of Independence, Fish Springs, Bishop and Little Lake.

November 28, 1872—Last and most remarkable of Indian troubles in California—the Modoc War—started when Capt. James Jackson and thirty-five United States soldiers, augmented by volunteers, sought to capture "Kientepoos," or Captain Jack, and a band of followers among the Modoc Indians of northeastern California, who had butchered an emigrant train and raided settlers indiscriminately. Jackson failed, losing a number of his men in the attempt. Soon larger forces of soldiers were sent against the Indians —at one time totalling a thousand men—but the savages, much fewer in number, evaded them, fleeing through the labyrinthine depths of the lava-beds and into mountain fastnesses. Treachery featured the Indians' warfare, and bungling strategy that of the whites. The latter were commanded by Gen. E. R. S. Canby. Numerous efforts to conclude peace proved fruitless, the penultimate one resulting in the murder of two of the peace commissioners, Rev. Eleazer Thomas and General Canby, and the wounding of a third, Albert Meacham. Temporizing no longer, the troops closed in on the Indians, captured Captain Jack and his lieutenants, tried them before court-martial and hanged them at Fort Klamath on October 3, 1873, thus concluding the war. Those executed were Captain Jack, Schonchin John, Black Jim, Boston Charley, Barncho and Sloluck. One hundred and fifty-three other prisoners were sentenced to exile on the Quaw-Paw Agency in Indian Territory. Casualties for the war on both sides are roughly estimated at one hundred killed and two hundred and fifty wounded.

June 2, 1873—Ground was broken for the first cable street railway in the world in San Francisco. The cable railway was devised by A. S. Hallidie, a San Francisco manufacturer of wire rope, and William Eppelsheimer, mechanical engineer, the first section being built on Clay Street, from Kearny to Jones. The railway was completed and started successful operation in September, 1873.

August 18, 1873—The first ascent of Mt. Whitney,

highest peak in continental United States (14,496 feet), was made by John Lucas, Charles D. Begole and A. H. Johnson. They tried unsuccessfully to name it "Fisherman's Peak," but in view of the fact that it had been previously seen in July, 1864, by a party of the California Geological Survey and named by them "Mt. Whitney" in honor of Josiah Dwight Whitney, chief of the survey, "Fisherman's Peak" was rejected. Clarence King attempted to climb the mountain in 1864 but failed, by a few hundred feet, to reach the summit.

February 12, 1874—San Benito County was created by legislative enactment from the northern and eastern portions of Monterey County. San Benito County in 1930 had a population of 11,311.

February 17, 1874—Modoc County was created by legislative enactment from a portion of Siskiyou County. Modoc County in 1930 had a population of 8,038.

June 17, 1874—Yosemite Valley was first opened to travel by wheeled vehicles upon completion of the Coulterville toll-road by the Coulterville and Yosemite Turnpike Company. In July of the same year, the Big Oak Flat Company completed its toll-road to the floor of the valley, and on July 22, 1875, the Mariposa road was finished. On March 26, 1895, Gov. James H. Budd signed a bill providing for the survey of a free wagon-road from Mariposa to Yosemite.

February 27, 1875—Romualdo Pacheco was inaugurated as twelfth American constitutional governor of California. Pacheco was the first California-born governor to assume this office after the American conquest. He was born at Santa Barbara October 31, 1831, went to school in the Hawaiian Islands, returned to California in 1843, was elected to the State assembly in 1853 and the State senate in 1861. He was State treasurer in 1863, and returned to the State senate in 1868. He was elected lieutenant-governor in 1871, and to the United States House of Representatives for the Forty-sixth Congress. He died at Oakland on January 23, 1899.

July 11, 1875—The Native Sons of the Golden West, a fraternal organization with membership restricted to males over sixteen years of age, "born in California or west of the Sierra Nevada Mountains after the 7th day of July, 1846," was organized in San Francisco. The Native Daughters of the Golden West, with similar purposes, but with membership restricted to the opposite sex, was organized at Jackson, September 25, 1886. Both societies have been exceedingly active in perpetuating interest in California's traditions and in preserving and restoring its historical antiquities.

August 26, 1875—The Bank of California was forced to close as a result of the unbridled speculation in Virginia City mines and mining enterprises engaged in with the bank's funds by the bank's president, W. C. Ralston. Ralston committed suicide the day after the bank closed. Later the institution was reorganized under the direction of William Sharon, and re-opened.

December 9, 1875—William Irwin was inaugurated as thirteenth American constitutional governor of California. Irwin was born in Ohio in 1827, and had been a college professor and editor of the *Yreka Union* before entering politics. He was generally regarded as an executive of mediocre talents. He died in San Francisco on March 15, 1886.

September 5, 1876—The first railroad connection between San Francisco and Los Angeles via the Southern Pacific Company was established when Charles F. Crocker drove a golden spike at the junction of the northerly and southerly advancing rails at Lang Station in Soledad Canyon, near Newhall.

July 23, 1877—General lawlessness and the growth of anti-Chinese sentiment in San Francisco, resulting on this date in a riot, the burning of one Chinese laundry and the destruction of several others, led to the revival of the Vigilance Committee, and the enlistment of six thousand reputable citizens in the cause of law and order.

September 12, 1877—Unemployment and the competition afforded by Chinese laborers caused California workingmen to organize the Workingmen's Party of California. Prime leader in the movement was Dennis Kearney, an Irish drayman who, in the course of a series of "sand-lot" meetings, enlisted thousands of recruits to the party. Principal objects were the exile of Chinese laborers, the partition of large land holdings, the transference of government from capitalistic interests to the people, etc. Kearney and his associates, with their inflammatory utterances, created a vast deal of agitation, some riots, and were jailed on occasion. Their adherents gained minor political offices, but the party was short-lived.

April 1, 1878—The city of Berkeley was incorporated. Founders of the present community may be regarded as Hall McAllister, R. B. Hammond, L. Herrmann and J. K. Irving, who in 1853 purchased a large parcel of the land constituting the site of the present city from Domingo Peralta, son of Luís Peralta who had been granted the land, as Rancho San Antonio, in 1820. Berkeley in 1930 had a population of 82,109, and an area of 9.50 square miles.

July 4, 1879—California's revised constitution, created by a constitutional convention assembled September 28, 1878, and subsequently ratified by the people, became effective. The constitution, revising the original one adopted October 13, 1849, provided new regulations for the election and conduct of the judiciary, new forms of taxation, more stringent regulation of banks, corporations and railroads, the operation of public schools, the establishment of towns and counties, etc. J. P. Hoge of San Francisco was president of the convention.

July 29, 1879—The University of Southern California was founded when property-owners, through Ex-Gov. J. G. Downey, O. W. Childs and I. W. Hellman, deeded three hundred and eight lots in West Los Angeles to trustees of the university, who included A. M. Hough, J. P. Widney, E. F. Spence, M. M. Bovard, G. D. Compton and R. M. Widney.

January 1, 1880—California's first State Railroad Commission, provided by the revised State constitution adopted by convention in November, 1879, was organized. Commissioners were: Joseph S. Cone, president; C. J. Beerstecker and George Stoneman.

January 8, 1880—George C. Perkins was inaugurated

as California's fourteenth American constitutional governor. Born in Maine, August 23, 1839, Perkins came to California at the age of sixteen, engaged in mining, purchased a store at Oroville, practiced law and later was one of the founders of the Arctic Oil Works, the Pacific Steam Whaling Company, and the West Coast Land Company. Perkins's administration was chiefly distinguished for the number of prisoners he pardoned from the State penitentiary, for which he was severely criticized.

December 1, 1881—The Southern Pacific Railroad, building easterly via Yuma and Southern Arizona and New Mexico, met the Texas Pacific Railroad at Sierra Blanca, Texas, thus giving California its second transcontinental railroad.

May 6, 1882—President Chester A. Arthur signed a bill suspending Chinese immigration to the United States for ten years, and denying the Chinese the right to become naturalized American citizens. Thus, with exclusion, was settled the Chinese problem in California.

January 10, 1883—George Stoneman was inaugurated as California's fifteenth American constitutional governor. Stoneman was born at Busti, New York, August 8, 1822, was graduated at West Point in 1846, and served in the Mexican War under Gen. Stephen W. Kearny. He came to California with Gen. A. J. Smith's command, went east to fight in the Civil War, was in the military service in Arizona in 1870, retired in 1871 to grow oranges at San Gabriel, became a member of the Board of United States Indian Commissioners and, finally, governor. He died at Buffalo, New York.

PART VI

GROWTH OF THE SOIL
(1885–1900)

GROWTH OF THE SOIL

(1885–1900)

THE madness of gold days couldn't continue in California for long. When the choicest fruits of the yellow harvest had yielded themselves to the adventuresome, mining became a complicated business, ill-suited to most of the Argonauts. Many of these returned to their native lands. Those who remained embraced other vocations.

In the meantime the fame of California had been bruited over the seven seas. It was a land of gold, true enough; but it was more; it was a land of fecund valleys and abundant mountains, where life was easy and the people gentle. The despoliation of natural resources that had proceeded so rapidly had carried its own lesson, and that was simply that all things must be conserved. The earth that is tilled faithfully, and the plant that is nurtured carefully, give well in return. Nature's laws are inexorable; one can't reap continually without doing some sowing now and then.

Thus there came to the land a new people. They were purposeful people. They were, in the main, farmers. They knew the earth and its capacity for growth. They knew that all wealth, all health and all enduring happiness and contentment spring from the soil, and here they found that the soil was good. They planted their farms, and they builded their homes, and they found an abiding peace. They served to check and balance the excesses of the '49ers; to give a more sober mien to the frivolities of the Spanish-Californians; to retrieve much that threatened to be lost, and to rehabilitate the moribund. They represented substantial and permanent values.

October 24, 1885—The Orange Growers Protective Union of Southern California was organized. This was the first coöperative marketing plan for citrus fruits, and was reorganized as the Southern California Fruit Growers Exchange in 1893.

October 27, 1885—The city of Fresno was incorporated. Fresno was established by the Southern Pacific Company in May, 1872. In 1930 it had a population of 52,513, and an area of 8.77 square miles.

November 9, 1885—The Atchison, Topeka and Santa Fe Railroad completed its line from Needles to Colton, and utilizing the Southern Pacific tracks from Colton to Los Angeles, began transcontinental service, thus giving California its third major transcontinental railroad.

February 14, 1886—The first full trainload of California oranges was shipped from Los Angeles to eastern markets. Previously, in 1877, a full carload had been thus transported. The orange was introduced into the State by the Spanish missionaries. First commercial production was instituted in 1841 by William Wolfskill in Los Angeles, and in 1853 Mathew Keller gave the movement impetus by importing orange seeds from Hawaii and Central America and planting an orchard near Wolfskill's. Commercial production of oranges in California in 1934 was valued at $90,791,538.

June 19, 1886—The city of Pasadena was incorporated. It is located on a part of the Rancho San Pascual, originally granted to Doña Eulalia Pérez de Guillen in 1827, and re-granted to M. Garfias in 1843. The modern city dates from the arrival of a group of Illinois and Indiana emigrants, known as the "Indiana Colony," under the leadership of T. B. Elliott and D. M. Berry, on January 27, 1874. In 1930 the city had a population of 76,086, and an area of 19.57 square miles.

June 19, 1886—The city of Glendale was incorporated. It is located on the site of Rancho San Rafael, first land grant in California. The ranch was given to José María Verdugo by Gov. Pedro Fages on October 20, 1784. The modern city dates from the partition of the rancho in 1870, when it was divided among some twenty-eight individuals. Its founders were Capt. C. E. Thom and Judge Erskine M. Ross. In 1930 Glendale had a population of 62,736, and an area of 19.21 square miles.

November 20, 1886—The city of Santa Monica was incorporated. The city is located on a portion of Rancho San Vicente y Santa Monica, granted December 20, 1839, to Francisco Sepúlveda. The present city dates from 1875, when it was laid out on land partitioned from the rancho by Senator John P. Jones and

Col. R. S. Baker. Santa Monica in 1930 had a population of 37,146, and an area of 8.00 square miles.

January 8, 1887—Washington Bartlett was inaugurated as the sixteenth American constitutional governor of California. Bartlett was born in Savannah, Georgia, February 29, 1824, arrived in California in 1849, was appointed first American *alcalde* or mayor of San Francisco, was subsequently publisher of the *San Francisco Journal of Commerce,* the *Stockton Journal,* the *San Francisco Evening Journal,* the *San Francisco Evening News* and, finally, the *True Californian.* He died from a lingering ailment, while still in office, at Oakland, September 12, 1887.

September 13, 1887—Robert W. Waterman, lieutenant-governor, was inaugurated as the seventeenth American constitutional governor of California on the death of Gov. Washington Bartlett. Waterman, a Republican, was elected lieutenant-governor at the same election where Bartlett, a Democrat, was chosen governor. He died at San Diego on April 12, 1891.

March 11, 1889—Orange County was created by legislative enactment from that portion of Los Angeles County lying south and east of a line running approximately along Coyote Creek. Orange County in 1930 had a population of 118,674.

January 1, 1890—The first Tournament of Roses was presented at Sportsman's Park, Pasadena, under the auspices of the Valley Hunt Club. Attendance was estimated at 2,000 to 2,500. Events included various races—foot, bicycle, burro and horse—and a parade of decorated carriages. A tournament in which five knights contested for prizes, and a football game, ended the festivities.

January 7, 1890—The first State Citrus Fair opened in Oroville. The fair included exhibits of oranges, lemons, limes, shaddocks, Japanese persimmons, raisins, nuts and preserved fruits, also green peppers, tomato vines, and strawberries in bloom.

September 25, 1890—Sequoia National Park was established by Act of Congress to preserve the best remaining specimens of Big Trees (*Sequoia gigantea*). The park was enlarged by an act of July 3, 1926, and now contains six hundred and four square miles. Noteworthy among its great trees is the General Sherman, 36.5 feet in diameter, and 272.4 feet high.

October 1, 1890—Yosemite National Park was established by Act of Congress to preserve a valley of unusual beauty created by glacial action, waterfalls, big trees, and wild life. The park contains 1,176.16 square miles, of which the valley proper occupies but eight square miles. The valley was discovered in 1851 by Maj. James D. Savage, who led an expedition into the Sierra in pursuit of marauding Indians. The Indians were known as "Yosemites," meaning, in their tongue, "grizzly bear." Dr. L. H. Bunnell, a surgeon who accompanied the expedition, suggested that the name be given to the valley.

October 1, 1890—General Grant National Park was created by Act of Congress to preserve remaining specimens of the Big Trees (*Sequoia gigantea*). The park is four miles square and contains the General Grant Tree, 267.4 feet high, and 40.3 feet in diameter.

December 30, 1890—A party of scientists, headed by Vernon Bailey, E. W. Nelson, and Frederick Vernon Coville, of the United States Department of Agriculture, left Keeler, California, to conduct the first botanical and zoölogical exploration of Death Valley. There resulted from this expedition voluminous reports on the birds, reptiles, fishes, insects, mollusks, trees and shrubs, cacti and yucca, etc., of the region, published by the department under the titles *Botany of the Death Valley Expedition,* and *The Death Valley Expedition.*

January 8, 1891—Henry H. Markham was inaugurated as the eighteenth American constitutional governor of California. Markham, a native of New Hampshire, served with the Union forces during the Civil War and settled at Pasadena in 1879. Markham made numerous profitable mining and real estate investments, served a term in Congress and there secured numerous appropriations for harbor development on the Pacific Coast. He died on October 9, 1923, in Pasadena.

March 11, 1891—Glenn County was created by legislative enactment from territory which had previously been included in Colusa County. Glenn County in 1930 had a population of 10,935.

October 1, 1891—Opening exercises of Leland Stanford Jr. University, founded by Mr. and Mrs. Leland Stanford as a memorial to their son, who died March 13, 1884, were held. The grant of endowment was made on November 11, 1885, by Mr. and Mrs. Stanford. David Starr Jordan was the first president of the university.

November 1, 1892—A board of United States Army engineers, engaged to examine the relative merits of Santa Monica Bay and San Pedro Harbor as the site of a port for the city of Los Angeles, reported to the Secretary of War favoring San Pedro, thus ending a long-standing conflict between Collis P. Huntington and Southern Pacific interests who favored Santa Monica, and Stephen M. White and others who supported San Pedro. The engineers' report was made public on January 7, 1893.

December 31, 1892—The San Antonio Light and Power Company began the transmission of electricity from its power station in San Antonio Canyon to Pomona, fourteen miles distant. This marked the birth of the hydro-electric industry in California, for it demonstrated the practicability of transmitting power over long distances. Previously, in 1882, a small hydro-electric plant at Etiwanda, built by George Chaffey, "father of water power" in California, had proved the feasibility of generating electricity from water power.

March 11, 1893—Riverside County was created by legislative enactment from territory previously included in San Diego and San Bernardino counties. Riverside County in 1930 had a population of 81,024.

March 11, 1893—Madera County was created by legislative enactment from that portion of Fresno County lying north and west of the San Joaquín River. Madera County in 1930 had a population of 17,164.

March 22, 1893—Kings County was created by legislative enactment from territory which had previously been a portion of Tulare County. Kings County in 1930 had a population of 25,385.

June 14, 1893—The panic prevailing throughout the United States descended upon Southern California with the failure of the Riverside Banking Company of Riverside, California. A week later four banks in Los Angeles, including the First National and the Southern California National, suspended, followed by similar failures in other localities. Recovery from the depression did not occur until 1898.

April 10, 1894—The first celebration of La Fiesta de Los Angeles began, continuing for four days. A parade was held on the opening day, presided over by the

"Queen of the Angels," and her attendants. This was the beginning of many such annual events, similar in character to New Orleans' noted Mardi Gras.

September 11, 1894—Pío Pico, last Mexican governor of California, died in Los Angeles. Pico was born at Misión San Gabriel May 5, 1801. He was the son of José M. and María Eustaquia Gutiérrez Pico, who had come from El Fuerte, Sinaloa, to Misión San Luís Rey in 1795. Pico became a member of the *diputación* or territorial assembly in 1828, and served continuously until 1842, save for a short period in January, 1832, when he occupied the governorship. He married María Ignacia Alvarado in 1834, was administrator of Misión San Luís Rey, 1834-1840, was granted Rancho Santa Margarita y las Flores in 1841, became acting governor February 22, 1845, and governor on April 18, 1846, fleeing from Los Angeles in August, 1846, when that city, then the capital, was captured by American troops.

December 25, 1894—The first East vs. West football game was held in San Francisco between Stanford University and the University of Chicago. The West was defeated by a score of 24 to 4. Five thousand people attended the event. Alonzo Stagg was the Chicago coach and the Stanford team was coached by Walter Camp.

January 11, 1895—James H. Budd was inaugurated as the nineteenth American constitutional governor of California. Budd was born in Janesville, Wisconsin, on May 18, 1851. He came with his parents to California in 1859 and settled in Stockton, where he was educated until he went to the University of California. He began the practice of law in 1874. He was a member of the House of Representatives in 1882 for one term, and refused to accept the office a second time when he was unanimously chosen by the delegates. He was also police and fire commissioner for Stockton in 1889. Budd was elected governor of the State in 1894 on the Democratic ticket. Upon his retirement from the governorship, he became attorney for the board of State harbor commissioners in San Francisco.

March 27, 1895—California's modern highway improvement program was inaugurated when Gov. James H. Budd signed a legislative act creating a "Bureau of Highways."

January 10, 1896—The first water shipment of crude oil by tank steamer, a cargo of 6,000 barrels, left Ventura, California, consigned to Rodeo in the especially built tank steamer *George Loomis*. The ship was built by the Pacific Coast Oil Company. First commercial production of oil started in California following the discovery in February, 1865, of petroleum in Pico Canyon, near San Fernando, by Mexican hunters. Production was sponsored by Gen. Andrés Pico, Col. E. D. Baker and Dr. Vincent Geleich. The oil industry was valued at more than a billion dollars in 1934, and its annual production totalled some $175,000,000.

December 12, 1897—The city of Long Beach was incorporated. First settlement was made in 1884, the community being known as "Willmore City." It was located on portions of the Ranchos Los Cerritos and Los Alamitos, the former, of five leagues, having been granted in 1834 to Manuela Nieto, and the latter, of six leagues, having been confirmed in 1834 to Juan J. Nieto. The modern city has a population (1930) of 142,032, and an area of 29.65 square miles.

May 27, 1898—President William McKinley appointed Col. Harrison Gray Otis, publisher of the *Los Angeles Times,* brigadier-general of California Volunteers in the Spanish-American War. General Otis was assigned to duty in the Philippines, where he remained until 1899, at which time he was honorably discharged.

January 4, 1899—Henry T. Gage was inaugurated as the twentieth American constitutional governor of California. Gage was born in November, 1853, in Geneva, New York, was educated in Michigan and began the practice of law in Los Angeles in 1877. He was elected governor in the November, 1898, elections on the Republican ticket.

April 26, 1899—Construction work was started on the breakwater at San Pedro by Helpmeier and New, contractors, which was destined ultimately to make Los Angeles Harbor first on the coast in volume of exports, and second in total shipping. The breakwater was completed in 1910.

April 3, 1900—The signing of a contract between George Chaffey, water resources engineer, and the California Development Company, which had been organized April 26, 1896 by Charles R. Rockwood, Samuel W. Ferguson and Anthony W. Heber, initiated active work for the reclamation and irrigation of Imperial Valley. Construction of canals was started immediately and colonists were encouraged to take up land under the Desert Land Act, through the quickly formed Imperial Land Company. The townsites of Imperial, Calexico, Brawley, Heber and Silsbee were laid out in the fall of 1900. In 1933 the area of the valley under cultivation was 368,209 acres, principal crops and their value being: Lettuce, $7,668,000; cantaloupes, $5,509,158; alfalfa, $1,714,079; honeyball melons, $1,697,788, and peas, $1,027,668.

PART VII

TURNING THE CENTURY
(1900–1935)

TURNING THE CENTURY

(1900–1935)

Most ludicrous and least significant in all of California's four hundred years are the decades surrounding the turn of the century. For a time all that had been gained in the way of individualism through the years of Spanish dominion, Mexican freedom and American liberality threatened to be lost. The caprices and the foibles of a people grown materially prosperous beyond ready measure menaced the Commonwealth.

An execrable architecture had displaced the simple, powerful, functional tradition of the Spanish-Californians. The honest fandango had given way to the pretentious and artificial salon. An affected "Culture" had been attained, and a forthright and a great culture had been sacrificed.

The interlude was a temporary one—the hectic and inexplicable fling of the profligate who, having profited well from life's tangibles, must dance with strange and degrading gods before advancing to newer and greater accomplishments.

But in its flight from reason California kept open the channels for a return. The inevitable recovery brought with it a new vision and a new perspective based on enlightening experience. In this twentieth century of the Christian Era it steps forward today on the record of the total of its past achievement and in the prophetic promises of the future, among the first rank of the States of the World.

March 31, 1901—The Southern Pacific Coast Line was opened. The first daylight limited trains made runs from Los Angeles to San Francisco, and from the northern city to Los Angeles.

August 1, 1901—The largest known tree in the world, a *Sequoia gigantea,* was discovered in the Sierra Nevada Mountains. Its circumference, as measured by John Muir, was one hundred and eight feet, one foot from the ground, and at six feet from the ground it measured ninety-three feet in circumference.

December 14, 1902—The S.S. *Silvertown* left San Francisco to begin laying the Pacific cable to Honolulu. The first message sent over the cable was from shore to the engineer of the *Silvertown* congratulating him on a successful landing and the splicing of the shore end of the cable.

January 7, 1903—George C. Pardee was inaugurated as twenty-first American constitutional governor of California. Pardee was born July 25, 1857, in San Francisco. He was educated in San Francisco and Oakland, and at the University of California. He then attended a medical school in San Francisco, and Leipzig University in Germany. He served on the Oakland Board of Health, the Oakland City Council, as Mayor of Oakland, and on the Board of Regents, 1899-1903, for the

University of California. He was a practicing oculist in Oakland from 1885 to 1903, at which time he was elected governor.

February 16, 1903—A bill making the *Eschscholtzia* (golden poppy) the California State flower was passed by the State Legislature. The poppy was classified first by Escholtz, a German botanist, from specimens gathered by his friend Adelbert von Chamisso, who accompanied Kotzebue's expedition to California in 1816.

May 4, 1903—A new California divorce law became effective, providing that the original decree of divorce shall be an interlocutory one, and that the final decree cannot become effective until one year thereafter.

May 12, 1903—The United States Indian Service moved 205 Indians from the Warner Ranch to the Indian reservation provided for them at Pala. Thirty-seven horse-drawn vehicles were required for the journey, which took two days. The move was made under the supervision of Indian Agent Wright, Commissioner Jenkins and Inspector Barnes. The Indians had protested the change by means of a petition addressed to the President of the United States, which was of no avail.

June 12, 1903—Announcement was made of the opening of an experimental station at Coachella for the introduction of date culture in the desert sections of California. The work was supervised by A. J. Peters, of the United States Department of Agriculture, and Prof. Arnold Stubenrauch, of the University of California.

July 4, 1903—The Pacific cable from San Francisco by way of Hawaii and Guam to the Philippines was opened when President Theodore Roosevelt sent, first, a message to the Philippines, and then a message around the world in twelve minutes' time.

August 31, 1903—A Packard automobile completed a fifty-two-day journey from San Francisco to New York City. This is believed to be the first time an automobile crossed the continent under its own power.

March 22, 1905—Gov. George C. Pardee signed a bill appropriating $5,000 to supply metallic guide posts to indicate the distance to, and the direction and location of, wells, springs, tanks, and other sources of water fit for drinking purposes in the desert sections of California.

July 11, 1905—Walter Scott, "Death Valley Scotty," completed his record-breaking trip from Los Angeles to Chicago on the Santa Fe Railroad. The trip was made in forty-four hours, fifty-four minutes, which cut the previous record by three hours and six minutes. Scott chartered a train consisting of Pullman, buffet diner and baggage cars for $5,000, with a bonus to the Santa Fe of $500 if the trip was made in less than forty-eight hours. The only passengers were Mr. and Mrs. Scott, two newspaper men, a magazine writer, and Scotty's mascot—a nondescript yellow dog wearing a thousand-dollar collar.

April 18, 1906—An earthquake shaking California from north of San Francisco to San Diego demoralized communication. In San Francisco a subsequent fire burned over an area of eight square miles, killed 250 people, wounded thousands, and caused property damage of $300,000,000.

July 19, 1906—The first bell marking El Camino Real was erected on the grounds of the Plaza church in Los Angeles. On the bell in raised letters are two dates —1769, the date of the founding of the first mission, and 1906, the date when the first bell was erected. The work was planned and supervised by the Board of Supervisors of Los Angeles County, and the Automobile Club of Southern California.

December 20, 1906—Active work began under the direction of Engineers Epes Randolph, H. T. Cory, and Tom Hinds in the final and successful effort to close the gap in the levee of the Colorado River which had been opened by Charles R. Rockwood in October, 1904, to increase the flow of water from the Colorado into the Imperial Valley and which, getting out of control, filled the Salton Sea and threatened to inundate the valley. The crevasse was finally closed on February 10, 1907.

January 9, 1907—James N. Gillett was inaugurated as twenty-second American constitutional governor of California. Gillett was born September 20, 1860, in

Viroqua, Wisconsin. He was educated in Wisconsin, and in 1881 was admitted to the practice of law there. He came to California in 1884 and settled in Eureka where he was city attorney for six years. He was State senator, 1897-1899, representative in Congress, 1903-1906, at which time he resigned. He was elected governor on the Republican ticket on November 6, 1906.

March 31, 1907—The S.S. *Ohio* arrived in San Pedro from Honolulu with two hundred and forty-seven passengers, the first regular passenger steamer ever docking in San Pedro from Hawaii. The voyage marked the beginning of an active commerce between these two ports. The vessel carried an excursion party from the Los Angeles Chamber of Commerce. As a result, $250,-000 of Hawaiian capital was pledged for the operation of a commercial steamship line between Honolulu and San Pedro.

August 15, 1907—Imperial County was created by legislative enactment from a portion of San Diego County. Imperial County in 1930 had a population of 60,903.

October 31, 1907—Gov. James N. Gillett declared the first of numerous legal holidays to prevent "runs" on California banks, which were the high-lights of the widespread panic of 1907-1908. Owing to the shortage of money, clearing-house certificates were issued in many localities. In San Francisco these totalled $13,040,000 in value.

January 9, 1908—Muir Woods National Monument in Marin County, California, was created by Presidential proclamation to protect an especially fine group of redwoods. The monument contains 426.43 acres.

January 16, 1908—Pinnacles National Monument in San Benito County, California, was created by Presidential proclamation to protect spire-like rock formations six hundred to one thousand feet high. The monument contains 8,908.39 acres.

February 4, 1908—Production of the first motion-picture for exhibition purposes was started in Los Angeles. Francis Boggs, director, and Thomas Persons, cameraman, rented a Chinese laundry at Seventh and Olive streets and there began to film a one-reel production, *Across the Divide*. Previously a motion-picture had been made on May 3, 1904, of Roy Knabenshue's old dirigible at Chutes Park, but as this was not made for commercial purposes, the motion-picture industry in California is considered to have been started in 1908.

June 16, 1908—The first taxicab operated west of Chicago was placed in service in Los Angeles. The first ten to be placed by the Taxicab Company, operated from the Western Motor Car Company garage. Earle

C. Anthony, manager, was responsible for securing them for the city. Four people could ride from any of the leading hotels to any of the theaters for thirty cents.

February 19, 1909—Gov. James N. Gillett signed the California Anti-Racetrack Gambling Bill introduced in the senate by Senator Walker of Santa Clara and in the assembly by Assemblyman Otis of Alameda. After a spirited battle between the proponents of the measure and the gambling interests, the bill was passed in the assembly by a vote of 67 to 10 and in the senate by 33 to 7. This was considered a real victory for the advocates of the bill, as it reached the governor with no changes to impair its effectiveness. The bill was repealed, and gambling on horse races was again legalized, by vote of the people at an election held July 25, 1933.

March 22, 1909—Gov. James N. Gillett signed a legislative act, ratified by the voters in November, 1910, providing for an $18,000,000 bond issue for the construction of California's first State highway system. By 1934 the first highway commission and its successors had created a State highway system aggregating 14,074 miles.

March 24, 1909—Gov. James N. Gillett approved the Direct Primary Law, an act providing for the choice by means of direct primary elections of United States Senators from the State of California, as well as for other city, county and State offices. The act was to take effect on and after June 1, 1909.

January 18, 1910—During the course of California's

first aviation meet, one of the earliest to be held in the United States, Louis Paulhan established a world record for sustained flight when he piloted a Bleriot monoplane from Dominguez Field, between Los Angeles and Long Beach, to the Santa Anita Ranch and back, a distance of forty-five miles.

October 1, 1910—The building of the *Los Angeles Times* was dynamited, killing twenty-one persons. James B. and John McNamara were convicted of the crime on December 5, 1911, after a sensational trial, in which they were defended by Clarence Darrow, who had been retained in their behalf by labor leaders.

January 3, 1911—Hiram W. Johnson was inaugurated as twenty-third constitutional governor of California. Johnson was born at Sacramento on September 2, 1866. He received his college education at the University of California, practiced law from 1899 to 1902, was corporation counsel for the City of Sacramento in 1899, and moved to San Francisco in 1902, where he lived until his election as governor on November 8, 1910, on the Republican ticket. He was re-elected on the Progressive ticket on November 3, 1914, inaugurated for his second term on January 4, 1915. He resigned from office March 15, 1917, to run for United States Senator. He has been serving in that capacity continuously since his election.

January 9, 1911—An amendment to the State constitution was filed with the Secretary of State providing for equal suffrage for men and women citizens of California, excluding Chinese, felons, idiots, insane people, or those unable to read the Constitution in the English language.

February 3, 1911—The Bear Flag, first raised on June 14, 1846, as the standard of the "California Republic," was adopted as the State flag by legislative enactment.

March 4, 1911—The first laws were enacted making it a misdemeanor for an operator of a motor vehicle to fail to render aid to any pedestrian struck, and likewise to operate any power vehicle under the influence of intoxicating liquor.

April 3, 1911—Gov. James N. Gillett approved the Initiative, Referendum and Recall Act, which provided for direct action by the people of the State of California by means of petitions and general elections with respect to legislation and elective officials. The same measure dealing with municipalities was approved by Gov. Gillett on March 14, 1911. On February 20, 1911, there was filed with the Secretary of State an amendment to the State Constitution, reserving to the people of California the power to propose laws, statutes and amendments, and to enact these at the polls independent of the Legislature, and also to approve or reject at the polls any act of the Legislature.

April 8, 1911—Gov. James N. Gillett approved the Workmen's Compensation Act, establishing the liability of employers for injuries or death sustained by their employees, and for compensation for the accidental injury of an employee. The act became effective September 1, 1911.

July 6, 1911—The Devils Post Pile National Monument in Madera County, California, was created by Presidential proclamation to preserve an area of remarkable geometrical rock exfoliations. The monument contains eight hundred acres.

October 10, 1911—California voters ratified a legislative enactment providing suffrage for women. The first woman in California to exercise the privilege of equal suffrage was Mrs. Sadie E. McLeod, wife of a Stockton publisher who, on November 14, 1911, cast her vote in a municipal election held to determine whether or not the city of Stockton should install and maintain an electric lighting system in the business district.

October 10, 1911—California voters ratified State constitutional amendments, placing in the hands of the people the authority to recall public officials, and the referendum to repeal or modify acts of the Legislature or other law-making bodies. Both measures, the Recall, and the Initiative and Referendum, passed by a three-to-one majority.

October 30, 1911—The constable of San Antonio township drew the first venire of women ever called for jury duty in California. Thirty-six names were drawn, all women, none of whom refused to serve. The trial was scheduled for November 2 in the Justice Court at Watts.

November 5, 1911—The first transcontinental airplane flight was completed by Calbraith B. Rodgers, from New York to Pasadena. The trip took forty-nine days. The total flying time was eighty-two hours, and the distance, 3,390 miles.

April 29, 1912—*The Mission Play*, foremost and longest playing of Western dramas, written by California's poet laureate, John Steven McGroarty, was given its premiere at the Mission Playhouse in San Gabriel.

May 15, 1912—The first pathfinding trip for a transcontinental highway from the Pacific to the Atlantic was started when a car, sponsored by the *Los Angeles Times,* left Los Angeles to explore the route. Coöperating in the venture was the Ocean-to-Ocean Highway Association. The route followed took the party through Yuma, El Paso, Dallas, Memphis, St. Louis, Chicago, Philadelphia, and thence to New York.

June 13, 1912—The Department of Commerce and

Labor announced a ruling upholding the action of the immigration board at San Francisco in detaining Japanese "picture brides." Nearly ninety per cent of Japanese women admitted to this country had been coming as picture brides, whose only proof of marriage was their likeness to photographs in possession of their "husbands."

May 19, 1913—The California Land Act was signed by Gov. Hiram W. Johnson, providing that aliens not eligible to citizenship are limited to rights specifically secured by treaty, thus prohibiting Japanese from ownership of agricultural land.

June 16, 1913—Gov. Hiram W. Johnson approved the Civil Service Act, providing for a general system for the employment of subordinate State employees based upon investigation as to merit, efficiency and fitness for appointment to and holding during good behavior of office, and employment under State authority and to create a Civil Service Commission with prescribed duties and powers. The act became effective August 10, 1913.

October 14, 1913—Cabrillo National Monument at San Diego, California, designed to preserve the first landing place of Juan Rodríguez Cabrillo in California in 1542, was created by Presidential proclamation. The monument is half an acre in area.

November 5, 1913—The Los Angeles Aqueduct, bringing water from the Owens River to Los Angeles, was completed. The project cost $25,000,000, and was under the supervision of Chief Engineer William Mulholland.

February 10, 1914—The *Great Northern,* first passenger liner to traverse the Panamá Canal, arrived at San Diego.

February 16, 1914—Silas Christofferson, San Francisco aviator, made the first air flight from San Francisco to Los Angeles, continuing on to San Diego the same day. Christofferson's three previous attempts to cross the Tehachapi Mountains had proved unsuccessful.

April 11, 1914—The Llano del Río Colony, a Socialist agricultural community, was founded on the Mojave Desert between Victorville and Palmdale, under the leadership of Job Harriman. The colony started with five members and attained a maximum of nine hundred resident members in 1917. Lack of capital and sufficient land for agricultural purposes caused the site to be abandoned and the colony moved to Stables, Louisiana, in the fall of 1917.

May 13, 1914—The first cargo of California products left San Pedro for the east coast via the Panamá Canal. The shipment was made on the S.S. *Isthmian* of the American-Hawaiian line.

January 1, 1915—The Panamá-Californian Exposition at Balboa Park, San Diego, was formally opened at dawn by a telegraphic signal dispatched by President Woodrow Wilson.

January 25, 1915—Regular telephone communication was permanently established between New York and San Francisco. Alexander Graham Bell talked with his assistant, Thomas W. Watson, in San Francisco, in the first conversation across the continent.

February 20, 1915—The Panamá-Pacific International Exposition formally opened at San Francisco, to commemorate the completion of the Panamá Canal. Exhibits were sent by countries all over the world, which was considered especially remarkable in view of the fact that war was raging in Europe at this time. The exposition closed December 4, 1915.

July 22, 1916—During a Preparedness Day parade in San Francisco a bomb exploded among spectators on Market Street, causing the death of six people and injury to twenty-five. Of labor leaders accused in the affair, Warren K. Billings was subsequently convicted and sentenced to life imprisonment, and Thomas Mooney received a death sentence, which on November 28, 1918, was commuted to life imprisonment by Gov. William D. Stephens, after intercession by President Woodrow Wilson.

August 9, 1916—Lassen Volcanic National Park was created by Act of Congress to preserve the only active volcano in continental United States, together with numerous hot springs and mud geysers. The park, with its subsequent additions now totals one hundred and sixty-three square miles in area. The volcano, Lassen Peak, is 10,453 feet high and was in frequent eruption between 1914 and 1917. The park is named for Peter Lassen, a pioneer of 1840.

September 15, 1916—W. F. Alder of Los Angeles demonstrated his invention for talking pictures to a group of Hollywood capitalists and motion-picture men. Mr. Alder's invention was patented and was the first to record sound on a "sound track" synchronized on the same film with the picture.

March 15, 1917—William D. Stephens was inaugurated as twenty-fourth American constitutional governor of California. Stephens was born on December 26, 1859 at Eaton, Ohio, where he received his high school education, taught school and read law. He was a member of an engineering corps on railway construction in Ohio, Indiana, Iowa and Louisiana, 1880-1887. He came to Los Angeles in 1887, engaged in the grocery business, 1902-1909; was mayor of Los Angeles, 1909; Congressman, 1911-1916, at which time he was appointed governor of California upon the resignation of Hiram W. Johnson, who went to the United States Senate. Stephens was elected governor of the State for the term 1919-1923 on the Republican ticket. He was admitted to the bar in 1919, and received a degree of L.L.D. from the University of Southern California in 1921.

September 5, 1917—The first contingent of the great American army in the World War, created under the Selective Service Act, was entrained at each examination district in California for the mobilization camp at American Lake, Washington.

July 25, 1918—Annette Abbott Adams became first woman United States District Attorney, serving in the northern district of California under appointment of President Woodrow Wilson. She occupied the office until June 26, 1920.

June 21, 1920—A severe earthquake wrecked a large part of Inglewood and rocked neighboring communities. Damage was estimated at $100,000, with one death reported and no injuries.

July 29, 1920—The first transcontinental air-mail flight from New York City to San Francisco was completed. On September 8, regular air-mail service was inaugurated between Mineola, New York, and Marina Field, San Francisco. Sixteen thousand letters were carried on the first regular flight.

May 7, 1921—Gov. William D. Stephens signed Assemblyman T. M. Wright's prohibition enforcement bill, which adopted for the State of California the provisions of the Volstead Act enacted by the United States Congress. This act provided for the enforcement by State administrative agencies, courts and law officers of the Eighteenth Amendment to the United States Constitution. The Wright Act was adopted by a mapority of 29,621 votes. At the general election in November 8, 1932, by a vote of two to one, California repealed the Wright Act and substituted a liquor control act contingent upon repeal of the Eighteenth (national prohibition) Amendment, which was effected December 5, 1933.

January 8, 1923—Friend W. Richardson was inaugurated as twenty-fifth American constitutional governor of California. Richardson was born in Michigan in 1865, came to California when very young and settled in San Bernardino. He was editor and proprietor of the *San Bernardino Times-Index,* then moved to Berkeley, where he edited the *Berkeley Daily Gazette.* He was president of the California Press Association, superintendent of State printing, 1911-1914; and State treasurer, 1914-1922. Richardson was elected governor on the Republican ticket November 7, 1922.

February 9, 1923—Gov. Friend W. Richardson signed a legislative concurrent resolution ratifying the Colorado River pact, providing for the division of the river waters between seven southwestern States.

May 2-3, 1923—The first transcontinental non-stop airplane flight was made by Lieutenants Kelly and Macready from New York to San Diego. The fliers covered the 2,516 miles in twenty-six hours, fifty minutes.

July 21, 1923—The first yacht race to Honolulu was held, with six boats leaving Santa Barbara at noon for the longest ocean race ever held as a sporting event. The six yachts were: *Diablo* (Santa Barbara Yacht Club), *Mariner* (San Francisco Yacht Club), *Viking IV* (Newport Harbor Yacht Club), *Idalia* (California Yacht Club), *Spendrift* (California Yacht Club), and the *Poinsetta* (California Yacht Club). This race is now held annually from Los Angeles Harbor.

August 2, 1923—Warren Gamaliel Harding, twenty-ninth President of the United States, died of acute gastritis in his suite at the Palace Hotel, San Francisco, during the course of a lengthy trip throughout the United States and to Alaska.

September 23, 1924—Three Los Angeles-made airplanes, commanded by Lieut. Lowell Smith, completed the first circumnavigation of the world by airplane at Clover Field, Santa Monica. The trip was made in six months.

June 29, 1925—A severe earthquake demolished the business district of Santa Barbara at 6:42 A.M. Seventeen deaths were reported and damage was estimated at $15,000,000.

November 21, 1925—Lava Beds National Monument, in Modoc County, California, was created by Presidential proclamation, to protect weird lava flows, including numerous caves. The monument contains 45,967 acres.

April 17, 1926—The first all-air mail and passenger service between New York and California was inaugurated when "Jimmy" James, pilot for the Western Air Express, landed at Vail Field, Los Angeles, from Salt Lake City. His flying time from Salt Lake City was five hours, ten minutes.

October 25, 1926—The campus site of the University of California at Los Angeles was dedicated at Westwood. Dr. Ernest C. Moore, director of U. C. L. A., Gov. Friend Richardson, and President Campbell of the University of California, were the principal speakers. On September 21, 1927, the first spade of earth for the new library building, the first to be constructed on the new campus, was turned by Dr. Moore.

January 4, 1927—Clement C. Young was inaugurated as twenty-sixth American constitutional governor of California. Young was born April 28, 1869, in Lisbon, New Hampshire. He came to California when he was a year old, lived in Butte County, was educated at San José, Santa Rosa and at the University of California. Young then became a teacher in a San Francisco high school, engaged in the real estate business from 1906 to 1927, was State assemblyman from Berkeley, 1908-1919, and speaker of the assembly, 1913-1919. He served as lieutenant-governor, 1918-1927, and was elected governor on the Republican ticket on November 2, 1926.

July 29, 1927—The California "gin marriage law" became effective. This law requires a three-day notice of intention to marry before the marriage license is issued, and was designed to prevent hasty marriages between couples under the influence of intoxicating liquor.

September 8, 1927—Seven fleet destroyers of the United States Navy went aground on Point Argüello. This mishap resulted in a loss of life to twenty-three sailors, and was attributed to faulty functioning of radio compasses and direction finders.

January 27, 1928—The Henry E. Huntington Library and Art Gallery at San Marino was opened to the public for the first time. This collection of rare books, manuscripts and paintings—one of the finest in the world—was made by Henry E. Huntington, Southern California traction magnate, and dedicated to the people of the State of California.

March 13, 1928—The Saint Francis Dam, located in San Francisquito Canyon, broke, flooding the valley of the Santa Clara River. More than four hundred lives were lost and the property damage was estimated at $30,000,000. Fifteen hundred persons were left homeless.

December 21, 1928—President Calvin Coolidge signed the Boulder Dam Act, providing for the construction of a dam in the Black Canyon of the Colorado to store 26,000,000 acre feet of water for irrigation and flood control purposes, and to develop 1,000,000 horsepower of electrical energy. Sponsors of the act were California's Representatives Ralph Swing and Senator Hiram Johnson.

March 15, 1930—The First International Pacific Highway Expedition, sponsored by the Automobile Club of Southern California, and headed by Chief Engineer E. E. East, left Los Angeles by automobile to survey the initial section of the route through Latin-America from Nogales to Puebla, Mexico.

July 7, 1930—Secretary of the Interior Ray Lyman Wilbur issued an order to Dr. Elwood Mead, Commissioner of Reclamation, to commence construction on Boulder Dam. Walker R. Young, construction engineer in direct charge at the project site, began staking out the railroad and construction road and laying out streets for the town. Surveys for the water supply system were also made. The original appropriation of $10,660,000 was made on September 17, 1930, at Las Vegas, Nevada. Secretary of the Interior Wilbur started preliminary work on Boulder Dam, giving it the name of "Hoover Dam." A silver spike was driven in a branch rail line. It was later pulled out and presented to Secretary Wilbur.

January 6, 1931—James Rolph, Jr., was inaugurated as twenty-seventh American constitutional governor of California. Rolph was born in San Francisco August 23, 1869. He was educated in San Francisco and engaged in the shipping business, general insurance and banking. Rolph was chairman of the Mission Relief Committee in 1906, president of the Mission Promotion Association, Shipowners' Association of the Pacific Coast, Merchants' Exchange of San Francisco, and a director of the San Francisco Chamber of Commerce. He was mayor of San Francisco for five terms, 1911-1930. Rolph was elected governor on the Republican ticket in November, 1930, and served until June 2, 1934, when he died at Riverside Farm in Santa Clara County.

January 17, 1931—The Second International Pacific Highway Expedition, sponsored by the Automobile Club of Southern California and headed by Chief Engineer E. E. East, left Los Angeles by automobile to survey the second section of the route through Latin-America, from Mexico City to San Salvador. The road, when finally built, will stretch from Alaska to Argentina.

March 1, 1931—Statues of Father Junípero Serra, California's apostle to the Indians, and Thomas Starr King, who saved California to the Union in the Civil War—selected by the Legislature as California's two most eminent citizens—were unveiled in National

Statuary Hall, Washington, D. C. The statue of Serra is the work of Sculptor Ettore Cadorin; that of King is by Haig Patigian.

March 11, 1931—The actual construction of Boulder Dam was authorized as Secretary of the Interior Ray Lyman Wilbur signed a document accepting the bid of the Six Companies, Inc., of San Francisco, to build the dam, powerhouse and appurtenant works for $48,890,995.

May 30, 1931—The coastwise steamer, *Harvard,* running between San Francisco and Los Angeles, went aground in a heavy fog at dawn at Point Argüello, "the graveyard of the Pacific." All passengers, four hundred and ninety-seven, and the crew were brought to Los Angeles Harbor by the United States cruiser *Louisville.* No lives were lost and no injuries suffered.

September 13, 1931—The Mission of San Diego de Alcalá, established in 1769 by Father Junípero Serra, after being restored, was rededicated.

September 30, 1931—California voters approved the issuance of bonds in the sum of $220,000,000 for the

Metropolitan Water District to provide for the construction of an aqueduct from the Parker Dam site to carry Colorado River water to various cities in Southern California.

May 13, 1932—The Board of Regents of the University of California accepted the gift tendered by Mr. and Mrs. W. K. Kellogg of Battle Creek, Michigan, of their eight-hundred-acre Arabian horse ranch, at Pomona. With the ranch were given ninety-five head of pure-blood Arabian horses, representing one-fourth of the Arabian horses outside of Arabia, and an endowment of $600,000 to continue the work of propagation and preservation of the Arabian horse strain.

July 30, 1932—Vice-President Charles Curtis opened the Tenth Olympiad at the Olympic Stadium in Los Angeles. The games were participated in by two thousand athletes from thirty-seven nations, and closed August 14, 1932.

January 8, 1933—Construction work was started on the Colorado River Aqueduct in Southern California by the Metropolitan Water District, under direction of General Manager and Chief Engineer F. E. Weymouth.

February 11, 1933—Death Valley National Monument in Inyo County, California, was created by Presidential proclamation to protect the numerous scenic and geological curiosities of the lowest and hottest valley in the United States. The monument contains 1,601,800 acres.

February 26, 1933—The first spadeful of earth was turned in the construction of the Golden Gate bridge at San Francisco. The bridge will be one mile long and will connect by direct highway San Francisco and the northern coast counties.

March 2, 1933—Gov. James Rolph, Jr., ordered a three-day bank holiday extended on March 4 for three more days to allow time for protective legislation to be devised. This action was necessitated on account of the failure of many banks in eastern States and consequent heavy withdrawals of cash from California banks.

June 27, 1933—By a three-to-one vote California voters elected delegates to a convention to ratify the Twenty-first Amendment to the Constitution of the United States, which repealed the prohibition, or Eighteenth, Amendment. The convention met at Sacramento, July 24, and ratified the amendment. The State Legislature in 1918 had ratified the Eighteenth Amendment, which became effective January 16, 1920.

July 21, 1933—Gov. James Rolph, Jr., signed the California 2½ per cent Sales Tax Law, to become effective on midnight of the same day. A tax was levied on all retail purchases, with the exception of purchases by governmental agencies of foodstuffs for charitable purposes, and gasoline, which already was subject to a State tax. The revenue was expected to be from $80,-000,000 to $100,000,000 biennially.

October 12, 1933—Alcatraz Island Penitentiary, long used by the War Department as a military prison, was transferred to the United States Department of Justice as a place of incarceration for vicious Federal prisoners.

June 2, 1934—Frank C. Merriam, lieutenant-governor, became twenty-eighth American constitutional governor of California on the death of Gov. James Rolph, Jr.

November 6, 1934—Gov. Frank C. Merriam, conservative Republican, defeated Author Upton Sinclair, Democrat, for governor of California in the most bitterly contested gubernatorial election in California's annals. Sinclair's campaign was based on a radical "Epic" ("End Poverty in California") plan providing for placing the unemployed in State operated industrial plants and on State-supervised farms, issuance of script as a medium of exchange, exemption of small home-owners from taxation, etc. Merriam received 1,138,620 votes, and Sinclair, 879,537 votes.

December 16, 1934—Construction work started on the All-American Canal, at a heading on the Colorado River, twelve miles north of Yuma, with appropriate ceremonies participated in by Gov. Frank Merriam, W. T. Whitsett, chairman of the Metropolitan Water District, and others. The canal, when completed, will run almost due west to a point west of Calexico and feed the secondary canals of the Imperial Irrigation

District. The canal will cost $38,500,000 and furnish water enough to irrigate 1,000,000 acres.

January 12, 1935—Amelia Earhart Putnam completed the first solo flight from Hawaii to California, a distance of 2,408 miles, which she negotiated in eighteen hours, sixteen minutes. She departed from Wheeler Field, Honolulu, and terminated her flight at Oakland Airport, Oakland. With the completion of the flight, Mrs. Putnam became: The first woman to make a successful flight across the Pacific; the first person ever to make a Pacific flight alone, either east or west; the first woman to fly both major oceans; the first person, man or woman, to do it alone.

February 1, 1935—Division gates were closed and storage of water started at Boulder Dam. It will take some three years to fill the huge man-made lake behind the dam, during which time construction work will be completed on the power-houses and other appurtenances.

INDEX

INDEX

A

Abella, Father Ramón, explores Sacto. and S. Joaq. rivers, 39, 42; founds S. Rafael mission, 42; dies, 72; biog., 72.

Adams and Co., 119.

Adams, Annette Abott, 180.

Adams, E., 114.

Aguirre, Juan Bautista, 20.

Alameda, Incorporated, 140.

Alameda County, formed, 115.

Alarcón, Hernando, x, 4.

Alcatraz Island, 20, 108, 188.

Alder, W. F., 179.

Alipas, Gervasio, 62.

All-American Canal, 189.

Alpine Country, formed, 132.

Altimira, Father José, 49.

Alvarado, Juan Bautista, leads revolt, 63; declared gov., 64; orders foreigners exiled, 67; grants New Helvetia, 69; dies, 71; biog., 71.

Alvarado, María Ignacia, 157.

Amador County, formed, 117; partitioned, 132.

American Party, 119.

AMERICANS, first in Calif., 30; first Amer. ship, 32; first Amer. settler, 41; Smith's arrival, 53; exiles in Graham revolt, 67; Wilkes explor. exped., 69; first emigrant train, 70; Amers. denied admittance to Calif., 75; seize Calif., 80.

Amurrio, Father Gregorio, 22.

Angel Island, 20.

Anian, Strait of, 3.

Anthony, Earle C., 171.

Anza, Juan Bautista, first exped. authorized, 18; reaches Calif., 19; second exped., 20; biog., 21.

Anzar, Father Antonio, 71.

Aquino, Father Tomás de, 7.

Argüello, Concepción, 37.

Argüello, José Dario, assumes governorship, 40; replaced, 41.

Argüello, Luís, explores Sacto. and S. Joaq. rivers, 42; explores Sacto. Val., 43; elected gov., 49; biog., 51.

Arnaz, José, 76.

Arrillaga, José Joaquín de, appointed gov., 31; replaced, 32; re-appointed, 36; dies, 40; biog., 40.

Arthur, Chester A., 146.

Ascensión, Father Antonio de la, 7.

Asumpción, Father Andrés de la, 7.

Atchison, Topeka and Santa Fe Railroad, 150.

Atherton, Gertrude, 37.

Auginbaugh, G., 140.

Automobile Club of Southern California, 168, 184, 185.

AUTOMOBILES, first transcontinental journey, 166; taxicabs, 170;

193